Teaching Integrated Arts i n the Primary School

Dance, Drama, Music and the Visual Arts

Anne Bloomfield

with John Childs

David Fulton Publishers
London

David Fulton Publishers Ltd
Ormond House, 26–27 Boswell Street, London WC1N 3JD
Website: http://www.fultonbooks.co.uk

First published in Great Britain by David Fulton Publishers 2000

British Library Cataloguing in Publication Data
A catalogue record for this book is available from the British Library

ISBN 1–85346–660–3

Typeset by Kate Williams, Abergavenny
Printed in Great Britain by The Cromwell Press Ltd, Trowbridge, Wilts.

Contents

Foreword

The current buzz word, whichever way you turn, is 'creativity'. There is no doubt that the arts are not the sole embodiment of this concept – scientists also need to be hugely creative to see beyond the current wisdoms.

However, the way we currently structure the curriculum – and more importantly measure children's success – in most subjects other than the arts, there is a tendency to stifle creativity rather than encourage it. As Professor Eisner said wisely in a recent lecture, 'without the arts, how are we to teach nuance, ambiguity or self-expression?' With so many subjects requiring a 'right' answer or correct spelling, it seems to me that only in the sphere of the arts are children allowed to be experimental and creative.

Teaching the arts in the primary school is the key to inculcating a lifelong habit. With a packed curriculum and many teachers lacking experience from their initial training, this book will be welcomed by all those who care about maintaining a secure base for the arts in our primary schools.

Penny Egan
Director, Royal Society for the Encouragement of Arts, Manufactures and Commerce
London, March 2000

Preface

Teaching Integrated Arts in the Primary School is about providing the joy of artistic experiences for children at an impressionable stage of their lives. Its points of reference are twofold – school-based teaching experiences and the theoretical framework supporting the nature of this involvement.

The impact of working with others has shaped my thinking and practice. I would like to thank sincerely the staff and students of the Nottingham Trent University for their particular roles and engagement with me in the arts, particularly the Primary PGCE 2000 group for the art work that illustrates some ideas in this book. Thanks are also due to Eppy, Tallulah, Charlie, Mortimer, Orson and Freddie for dancing and making music for the photographs, and Hannah and Lauretta for their delightful prints.

In attempting to comprehend the changes in educational thought and practice, and the various theoretical frameworks for the arts – one of my principal areas of research – I acknowledge guidance from Professor Alan McClelland, Miss J. B. Graham, Professor Gordon Bell, Dr Peter Abbs and Professor Bernard Harrison, each of whom in their special way has provided intellectual nurture, challenge and invaluable support.

Anne Denman and Don Barry Bloomfield have kindly supplied the photographs and Jane Streeter of the Bookcase, Lowdham, gave practical help in compiling resource information.

I am especially delighted that John Childs agreed to bring his considerable expertise to produce the chapter on music and thank him most sincerely.

Anne Bloomfield
Nottingham Trent University
March 2000

CHAPTER 1

The Integrated Arts Mode

REDEFINING THE ARTS CURRICULUM

The philosophical foundation for teaching integrated arts in the primary school is based on the belief that aesthetic and creative education is the entitlement of every child and that the nature and quality of the provision determines the distinctiveness of cultural life and academic performance in school. As a model for the new millennium, the integrated arts mode accords dance, drama, music and visual art a collective, central and pivotal role in primary education and demonstrates that when children experience the arts from an integrated approach their learning in the humanities, sciences, technology, literacy and numeracy is complemented and enriched. Children's natural enthusiasm for the arts, as major and valid sources of knowledge, is nurtured from the first day at school and their motivation and commitment is maintained throughout their primary years.

Rationale for the integrated arts mode reflects the developmental stages in the child's creative and artistic growth enabling teachers to nurture the *creative self* of the child, to facilitate the genesis of children's ideas and to help manifest the genius of their expression. It promotes individual achievement and provides the foundation for a lifelong interest and participation in the arts. Teaching approaches and learning experiences advocated for children incorporate independent linear programmes of study in the main subject areas of dance, drama, music and visual art, but also include the exciting possibilities of exploring the integrative nature of these disciplines. Although dance, drama, music and visual art possess their own epistemological knowledge areas, there are elements which overlap. The new millennium model recognises cognitive and affective modes of learning and the power each has upon the other as experienced by children studying the wide range of National Curriculum subjects. Unity of teaching and learning occurs because of the vibrant interaction of arts disciplines which are strengthened when collaboration and mutual support for, and from, other curriculum subjects takes place.

The new definition encourages a change of attitude towards the role and status of the arts in the primary school curriculum and places them in a context as the fourth 'R' alongside the traditional three 'Rs' of reading, writing and arithmetic.[1] Above all, the reaffirmation of the arts curriculum in the primary school denotes recognition of a number of important factors which are presented in Figure 1.1. Children are recognised

---

1. The term fourth 'R' is used by G. H. Bell (1998) in 'Arts education and the European dimension', in Bloomfield, A. (ed.) *The Artistic Experience*, Aspects of Education No. 55, University of Hull.

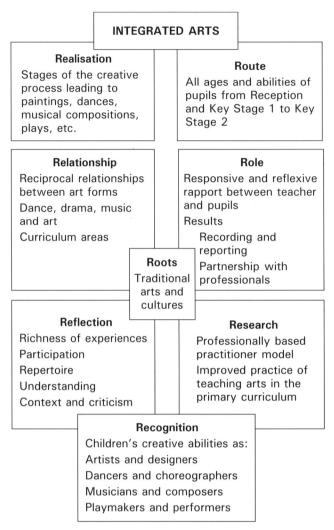

Figure 1.1   The reaffirmation of the arts in the primary school.
Mapping out the fourth 'R' in the new millennium model

as creative artists in their own right, with ideas and abilities that go beyond stylistic copies of adult work – this is a continuous route throughout the school years. From the spring-board of the nursery, or Reception class, there is a clearly focused programme extending through Key Stages 1 and 2 leading children towards proficiency, self-discipline and artistic control. There is recognition of the common processes that take place as children transform their ideas into the reality of artifacts such as paintings, dances, musical compositions or short plays. This practical realisation of their ideas recognises that children are artists in their own right and, importantly, the arts curriculum is conceived as a whole, acknowledging the distinctive art forms and the technical methods each require, but celebrating the reciprocal relationships and commonalities that are shared.

   The understanding of the roots of the arts as cultural forms recognises the links between creativity and traditional arts from around the world, past and present, and also represents how children are taught to reflect upon their own work and that of others as a natural outcome of rich experiences. Children's individual roles and their relationship with their teacher is highly valued. The process of professional development is the way in which teachers can explore their own professional practice, through sharing ideas, working together and recording the progress of their pupils. This shift in focus, reinstating the arts to the centre of learning for children, is intended to empower pupils and teachers providing a greater degree of flexibility and individual autonomy in the way in which the National Curriculum orders are interpreted. Legislation of the National Curriculum 2000 (DfEE & QCA 1999) facilitates and maximises the teaching and learning potential of the arts curriculum for the new millennium. All children, whatever their background or aptitude, have the ability to express themselves successfully through the arts, gaining confidence and a new means of accessing other areas of the curriculum.

Recognition, therefore, denotes the important role of the arts in the primary curriculum as valid routes of learning, not only as art forms in their own right, but as arteries that invigorate other fields of learning. The purpose of this book is to encourage successful, rewarding and confident teaching of the arts by providing a working framework that enables teachers to transform their ideas into the reality and joy of success and professionally rewarding practice.

THE TEACHING AND LEARNING FRAMEWORK FOR THE ARTS

An education in and through the arts is based upon the level of understanding, knowledge and skills that are acquired by children and which are experienced in an imaginative and creative way. Vital for individual achievement is the method of teaching and the teacher's own knowledge of the subject that is being taught. A special, dynamic and sensitive relationship exists between what the teacher knows, how the teacher provides an appropriate learning environment, and how the child responds to what is taught. The personal and sensitive quality of the arts means that the pupil's experience is a highly valued part of the learning process. Equally, although creative thought and independent action are desirable components in the art-making process, understanding the nature and context of the artifact by teacher and pupil is also important especially as an artifact acts as a vehicle through which cultural values are transmitted. The teacher's role is conceived as being interactive and responsive since feeling secure and gaining confidence are key issues for both the teacher and the pupil. This grows from an understanding of the knowledge areas of individual art forms and how they are to be applied.

The teaching and learning framework for the arts has been designed as a principal plan that recognises distinctive and interrelated areas of study in each major art form – dance drama, music and visual art – which are part of the primary school curriculum.[2] Teaching and learning principles are based on the ways in which children acquire knowledge, skills

2. The seminal model for the knowledge areas in the integrated arts was first presented for dance by the author in Bloomfield, A. (1985) 'A short treatise on the establishment of the quantum of knowledge in dance', in Bloomfield, A. (ed.) *Creative and Aesthetic Experience*, Aspects of Education No. 34, University of Hull. A complementary curriculum framework, incorporating language arts and media has been developed as an aesthetic field by Peter Abbs (1987) 'Towards a coherent arts aesthetic', in Abbs, P. (ed.) *Living Powers*. Lewes: The Falmer Press.

and understanding of dance, drama, music and visual art, and interrelated experiences through four types of engagement:

• art-making as a process
• realising through art by producing an artifact
• critical responses to the arts as process and product
• contextual understanding of art.

Firstly, art-making includes all the participatory experiences or practical engagement of children as they learn how to dance, to paint, to write, or to compose music. Secondly, as children progress through the school year their acquaintance with each art form deepens. They acquire knowledge which is synonymous with the level of their experience or repertoire. Thirdly, the practical experiences of the arts are supported by the ability to discuss or write about works of art, either dances, plays, paintings or pieces of music. These may have been produced either by children or professional artists. This area of understanding is referred to as propositional knowledge because it reflects the pupil's understanding of the meaning, action or symbolism inherent in the arts. Fourthly, discovering about the social, cultural or historical aspects of the arts means that children can refer to books, recordings, artifacts, videos and CDs in order to broaden their horizon and deepen understanding of their own work. Finding out about the arts in this way encourages children to acquire contextual knowledge.

The richness of an arts education is provided when children acquire knowledge and understanding through these four recognised routes since the understanding of one area enhances the understanding of another:

• participation – children's knowledge of how to paint, dance, write and make music
• repertoire – children's knowledge through experience and collecting their work
• critical skills – children's knowledge of the qualities and special nature of the arts
• contextual skills – children's knowledge of the historical, social, and cultural worlds that inform their work.

These areas are interrelated in some way or other, and each adds to the children's holistic understanding of the arts.

Participation through active engagement in art-making is based on children's ability to cope with its various technical aspects and the way in which this helps to fashion or create the artifact, for example, the manner in which children learn to draw and produce drawings. The collection of artifacts constitutes the repertoire, and may include drawings in a sketchbook; dances composed by or country dances learned by the class; songs they have learned to sing; and musical compositions, such as short percussion suites which children have learned and continue to perform. Over the academic year one class will have several different and varied artifacts as part of their repertoire, and each year of their school life should become the launching pad for the new aspirations of the following year's work.

Acknowledging that children are artists in their own right means that as individuals, or collectively as a class, they produce artifacts – paintings, sculptures, dances, plays – and in so doing engage in all the complexities that this entails. Creating an artifact draws upon inspiration, solution-seeking skills and decision-making skills that go beyond the acquisition of technical skills. For example, in dance the ability to execute a sequence of movements based on stepping and turning demands technical control and skill, but placed within the context of a dance also requires creative understanding. Teaching integrated arts in the primary school requires that children gain understanding of art-making processes and that they are able to recognise and value a finished work. The way in which their conceptual understanding of the arts goes beyond the confines of their own classroom depends upon the access and exposure they have to information and artifacts, including reproductions, from outside sources and visits. In this manner they will become familiarised with the context of the arts.

The knowledge, skills and understanding of the arts within the National Curriculum 2000 include participation, repertoire, critical and contextual skills, and requires that primary school pupils know:

- how to execute the skills required for art-making
- how to create artifacts
- how to analyse and understand the process inherent in production of the artifact
- how to observe and criticise artifacts
- about the arts in relation to the time and place of the art-makers and the artifact.

Figure 1.2 represents the child's role in acquiring and experiencing these major areas of artistic understanding, and provides some insight into the complexity of the processes

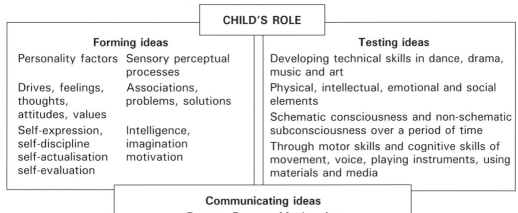

Figure 1.2   The artistic experience of children

involved from forming ideas, testing them out, making artifacts through which the ideas are communicated to the world, and then how the child learns to respond to the art works.

The reaffirmation of the arts in the primary school also relates to the teacher's role in meeting requirements and facilitating learning in the key areas of creating, realising and responding to art works, whether produced by the children or selected received works of art.

- *Creating* – refers to the manner in which the teacher guides the pupil through processes of making the dance, musical work, play, or painting, etc.
- *Realising* – refers to the way in which the teacher guides the pupil towards the emergence of the artifact or product which can be the dance, the poem, the song, the sculpture, etc.
- *Judgement* – refers to how the teacher responds to the artifact through critical evaluation and assessment including the way in which s/he responds towards the work the pupils have produced and the manner in which the pupils are taught to appraise their own work and that of others.
- *Context* – refers to the way in which the teacher excites interest in the cultural and historical aspects of the arts providing information about the where, why, and when of artists and their work.

Figure 1.3 is an overview of the teacher's role in this teaching and learning process, indicating how teachers help children to form and test their ideas through constructive teaching. It shows how teachers help the children to communicate through their art work, to gain understanding and insight of processes and finished works by developing their critical skills acquired through a variety of means that should be at the disposal of schools. Read in conjunction with Figure 1.2, this diagram shows the reciprocal relationship that exists between teacher and child and between other children in the class.

ARTISTIC AND AESTHETIC ASPECTS

The reaffirmation of the arts in the primary school recognises the interactive processes that occur between teachers and children during lesson time, when each shares an artistic vision of what an outcome will be, whether using paint, voice, instrument or, in the case of dance, movement. The teacher's role is always supportive, but the approach and style can vary from the didactic, interventional and contemplative. Throughout, the teacher is sensitive to individual needs and understands that the nature of the activity and the outcome will reflect children's own creativity and artistry since the art works produced – perhaps a painting, a dance or a piece of music – will reflect their individual perceptions of the world captured in symbolic form. The rich variety of experiences encountered by children through the processes of creating, realising, responding, and acquiring contextual understanding, draws upon cognitive and affective responses and activates their aesthetic sensibilities. The quickening of the children's aesthetic sense arises through the awareness of feelings which occur in response to producing or viewing a particular art form. For example, excitement at watching a play, feeling sad and solemn when dancing to music with those qualities, or feeling frightened at the sight of a particular painting.

TEACHER'S ROLE	
Helping children to form their ideas	**Helping children to test their ideas**
Stimulating and motivating creative thought and action, visualising and imagining, supposing and explaining, thinking in terms of moving, thinking in terms of looking, thinking in terms of listening, thinking in terms of speaking, thinking in terms of feelings, using appropriate words. Exploring ideas through techniques of dance, drama, music and art.	Guiding, suggesting, intervening, discussing, demonstrating, questioning. Explaining to children as they engage in creative thought and action. Applying techniques and skills of dance, drama, music and art. Facilitating and resourcing, enriching experiences, extending the use of artistic terminology.

Helping children to communicate their ideas

Integrated Arts

Dance   Drama   Music   Art

Guiding, supporting, appraising, discussing, valuing the children's artifacts – dances, plays, musical compositions, art display, etc.

Using an artistic and aesthetic vocabulary.

Assessing, recording and reporting as children build up their repertoire.

Helping children to respond to the arts

Offering emotional and intellectual experiences through which children understand, in a meaningful way, the nature of the arts.

Offering resources for the arts, arranging visits to galleries, theatres, museums, heritage sites, concerts, working with professional artists, and having access to film, video, Internet resources.

Equipping children with criteria for judgement of art works relative to stages of understanding.

Applying the vocabulary acquired through children's 'doing' to viewing and listening.

Expecting children to write about and read about art and artists, dancers, writers, musicians.

Figure 1.3   The teacher's role in facilitating integrated arts for children

Aesthetic education, as a revelation of education in and through the arts, is implicit in each of the four stages of the pupil's involvement of art-making through creating, producing the artifact, making judgements of works of art and exploring and gaining understanding of the context of the arts. These processes relate to the four art forms of dance, drama, music and visual art. Through the reaffirmation of arts, the primary school curriculum provides opportunity for children's aesthetic education to flourish by acknowledging the interrelationship between creating, realising, making judgements and knowing about contexts. The fourth 'R', in advocating an integrated approach, recognises that dance, drama, visual art and music are grouped collectively within the curriculum and establishes the circumstances through which interaction and rebound will occur.

Dynamic interplay between the arts may take place at different stages within each art form, for example, the process of creating a dance may occur using a finished musical composition. A finished painting may generate new ideas for music or dance. Similarly, other types of interaction will pass between their broader historical and global contexts, so that traditional art forms of a particular cultural group, perhaps American Indians or Tudor Britain, whether costume, music, portraits, or dances, can relate to the pupil's own creativity. The reaffirmation of the arts in the primary school is a pragmatic and practical exemplification of this theory and is based on the teacher and the pupil's understanding of the nature of each discipline and the way in which they relate to each other.

Dance, drama and music are performing arts and owe their existence to the element of time. In contrast, visual art and design have timeless qualities. Once the art-making process has passed and the art work has been completed it remains vested in time. Each of the arts is uniquely distinctive, and it is of the utmost importance that teachers allocate specific focus time to each discipline. Teaching integrated arts in the primary school advocates following programmes of study in separate disciplines as well as teaching lessons where integrative learning takes place. Although it is possible to combine two areas successfully within a lesson – for example the rhythmical aspects of dance and music where they occur indivisibly – it would necessitate building upon prior experiences of dance and music lessons containing the study of rhythm as the main area of learning. Table 1.1 shows the major elements of dance, drama, music and visual art, revealing the distinct and unique qualities and the shared attributes of each.

Table 1.1 Elements of the arts

Dance	Drama	Music	Art
Time – *performed*	Time – *performed*	Time – *performed*	Time – *concretised*
Visual – *spectacular*	Visual – *spectacular*	Visual – *spectacular*	Visual – *spectacular*
Kinaesthetic – *symbolic through gesture technique – body*	Kinaesthetic – *symbolic representation of gesture technique – body, speech*	Kinaesthetic – *practical skills, instrumental technique – instruments*	Kinaesthetic – *practical skills, implemental technique – implements tactile*
Rhythmic – *movement*	Rhythmic – *voice movement*	Rhythmic – *vocal and instrument*	Rhythmic – *visual through design/pattern*
Silent	Oral – *speech sound/mood*	Oral – *singing organisation of sounds*	Silent
Aural – *interpretation of music*	Aural – *interpretation of texts*	Aural – *interpretation of musical sounds and scores*	Silent

CHILDREN EXPERIENCING THE ARTS

Drama is a performance art using movement and speech. The method advocated within the context of the integrated arts is one that prepares the child as playmaker and performer. Children acquire a repertoire of drama over each school year that includes examples of play-making and interpretation. They use voice and movement, sometimes simultaneously, or separately as in mime or spoken dialogue. A systematic approach that incorporates games and whole class or group activities on drama based tasks will utilise improvisational movement and speech both as processes of acquiring drama skills and as the means of creating and interpreting play scripts, written scenarios or stories. Children's full participation in drama is based on their ability to speak, read, listen, and move in a creative and expressive way, shaping ideas in the same manner as the playwright uses the dimensions of space and time to bring characters alive on the stage.

Drama, as part of the English curriculum provides a rich source for speaking, reading, and listening. The dance lesson will provide the movement skills of body control and management and provide children with an understanding of the symbolical use of the body which they can apply in dramatic contexts. Movement in drama uses the child's ability to act out situations that may include taking on the role of another character. Children require to have confidence in the use of the voice, approached from the perspective of dialogue and interactive conversation or associated with drama games and improvisation. Structured improvisation based on an issue or a story can form the basis of the creative dimension of the spoken word, the inventive side of drama. Teaching approaches, as outlined in Chapter 2 ('The Drama Mode'), provide ideas ranging from voice plays, interpretations of Shakespeare, mime and dance drama. Critical awareness – by observing, discussing and writing about what was seen and heard, and what was experienced by the participant – completes the cycle.

Drama is akin to dance in terms of mime and story, and to music in terms of voice, rhythm and mood. Visual awareness in terms of spatial understanding and design provide links with art. Equally, the making of costume and properties for use in classroom and hall utilise design and making skills. Puppets and masks are a valuable and much loved aspect of dance and drama and are also means by which children express their understanding of themselves and the world.

Dance is brought alive when children perform movements in a meaningful artistic way. Their mastery and understanding of the art form is based upon the interpretation of movements that belong to a gestural symbolical language. Creative dance in education follows a system that, as a form of communication and expression for children, is based on a codification that they can understand and perform but which offers an intellectual, emotional and physical challenge while also presenting opportunities for social interaction. A thematic approach based on the synthesis of movement through simple patterns, sequences and dances as detailed in Chapter 3 ('The Dance Mode') is advocated. A conceptual interpretation of the elements of movement expressed instrumentally and rhythmically has great meaning for children. The expressive language of dance has similarities, in terms of steps and choreographic forms, with traditional dances of existing cultures and these enriching experiences ensure that the opportunities for children and teachers are exciting and varied.

Dance, as part of the integrated arts approach, enables children to acquire dancing skills as they progress through the primary years, awakening their sense of bodily intelligence. They understand how to move in an aesthetic and artistic way through the notion of embodiment. The use of the imagination, mental cognition and feeling are part of the kinaesthetic mode which empowers children to think and express ideas through every fibre of themselves. Creativity in dance commences from an idea or stimulus which begins to take on observable form as children work through the ideas in their dance lessons. They visualise, experiment, observe others as they respond to the teacher's guidance.

They transform images into realities by use of body shape, spatial patterns and pathways, and interpretation of musical rhythms. By dancing alone or with others, it is through the medium of movement that the dance emerges. Once performed it is practised, perfected and remembered. At that point it enters the repertoire of finished dances and can be performed for others to watch. Primary school children enjoy building up a diverse repertoire which includes various types of dances. The nature of dance is such that it can be likened to music in terms of rhythm and melodic interpretation – some dances arise from improvising to music and share the same organising structure. It is similar to drama in terms of mime and story, and to art in terms of spatial configuration as depicted in the choreographic patterns and the forming and reforming of group shapes. Through dance, children express their understanding of themselves and the world as they perceive it.

Music brings great joy to children, and whether using the voice or playing instruments, it offers a unique mode of experience through which they can both receive and express ideas and feelings, thus cultivating auditory intelligence. The emotional aspects of music and its power of visual imagery, whether stimulated though personal performance or listening to recorded or live performances by others, gives it a special dimension. Chapter 4 ('The Music Mode') provides a developmental approach that incorporates music-making, listening and appreciating, and is appropriate for children in primary schools as they build up a musical repertoire through exploring the world of sound.

Children of all abilities are drawn into the creative process of music-making and learn the skills of producing sounds with rhythmic, melodic, and tonal qualities. In order to achieve this they must acquire instrumental skills, whether using percussion instruments, selected tuned instruments, electronic instruments, or even other sound-producing objects that effectively transmit a precise nature of sound required for specific circum-stances. The ability to vocalise and use the voice creatively adds further depth to compositional studies. The received works of music, appreciated through listening or interpreted through performance, provide an additional dimension to the music curricu-lum. Interpretative skills of responding to musical works through playing is also linked to the child's level of musicianship and the ability to read a score. Music through the primary years will include aspects of recording and reading simple forms of musical notation. Programmes include reading and writing a score as appropriate to specific age ranges.

As in the case of dance and drama, primary school children will derive personal pleasure from compiling an exciting and stimulating musical repertoire. This means creating various types of musical pieces, which, analogous with dance, will range from pure musical forms and representational music. Pure music forms are sound studies that emerge from experiments in sound-making for its own intrinsic self. Through these experiences, children acquire a sensitive understanding of the nature of sound and the instrument that produces the sound. They derive pleasure from the sound patterns they produce, the melodic line, the rhythm, pace and metre, the relationship of silence and sound, and the way in which sounds evoke moods and feelings. Whether working alone, with a partner, in a small group or with the whole class as the orchestra, children make music with conviction and purpose.

Using a visual stimulus, children can create sound pictures, a useful transition to the realms of representational composition. In using the cantata form, children can use instruments and voice to make a sound story and through the use of sound patterns or musical motifs, they are able to express the ideas and emotions of the characters and events of selected stories or plays. Once created, as in the case of dance and drama, the musical piece must be practised, perfected and remembered. At that point it enters the musical repertoire. As previously stated, the skills of critical awareness complete the cycle.

The nature of music is such that it is related to dance in terms of rhythm and melodic interpretation – some musical phrases can arise from following dance sequences and use the same organising structure. It is akin to drama in terms of mime and story and the evocation of mood, plot and character. It uses art and design for visual imagery and patterns, sound pictures, and for masks and puppets when working towards performance. Music is organised and taught according to thematic principles based on the constituent elements of sound through which children express their understanding of themselves and the world. Choices from the repertoire of western music and resources reflecting the diversity of sounds from around the world make it possible for teachers to compile a stimulating music library.

Visual art is the way in which children express and communicate their ideas and feelings through the use of a wide range of materials. Their perceptions of the world are depicted through mark-making and image-making acquired when they are guided through the diagnostic processes of drawing, painting, modelling and constructing. Exploration of, and familiarisation with, materials and media have tangible outcomes in the form of paintings, collages, computer graphics, drawings, and printings as well as sculptural constructions, pottery, papier mâché and mod-rock (a plaster-impregnated fabric bandage that comes in strips), not to mention the infinite possibilities of mixed media. Realisation means the emergence of an artifact, a finished piece of work that has taken thought and skill and represents the best the child can do at that point in time. At a practical level, the range of materials, technical skills and modes of expression are diverse and an education in and through visual art in the primary school is founded on the child's natural curiosity of the visual world and the way in which it is recorded. The teacher excites this curiosity and teaches the necessary skills to empower children to record their ideas and feelings, culminating in finished works. A carefully constructed programme of study embraces investigating and making at a personal creative level which is the most powerful means by which the child ultimately begins to grasp critical understanding and the wider issues of cultural context. The range and systematic approaches for the teaching of visual art is outlined in Chapter 5, 'The Visual Art Mode'.

The visual art programme, as part of the integrated arts approach, requires that children obtain art based skills as they progress through the primary years. Their aesthetic understanding of visual art, both in terms of the work produced by themselves, their peers and looking carefully at the received works of art, is based on the concept of the 'intelligent eye', the cultivation of which encompasses the use of the imagination, mental cognition, and feeling. Creativity in visual art, as in dance, drama and music, commences from an idea or stimulus which begins to take on observable form as children work through the processes of visualising, experimenting in their sketchbooks, perusing through resources that the teacher has prepared for them, and engaging in constructive discussion with their friends and the teacher. Images in art are characterised through such aspects as line, shape, tone, shading, depth, relationship, form, volume, spatial relationships as well as colour and texture. Understanding the meaning of these terms and their use, either in relation to informing actions or informing critical discussion, is an important aspect of effective teaching. For example, at Key Stage 1 the children may be using charcoal for observational drawing of sea shells. The way in which they record what they see in terms of clarity of line, thickness, delicacy, highlight and shading is part of the sense of using a stick of charcoal and knowing how the effects are achieved – how the stick of charcoal is held, what pressure is exerted, how textures can be made. The implementation of ideas through the stick of charcoal is acquired through practical experiences. Conversation between the children and the teacher will ensure that children develop this understanding, which can be endorsed at another time through discussion of what other children had achieved – in this instance, analysing what was viewed in order to comment about a technical aspect that conveyed artistic meaning.

Over the duration of the school year, a primary class will amass a veritable collection of artifacts which the children have produced, some of which will be individual pieces while others will be joint efforts produced either as a result of group work or as an ongoing activity representing the efforts of each pupil. For example, a piece of weaving or a model in which designing, construction and painting have been undertaken as a class project over a period of time. Children can each have a portfolio or folder for individual pieces of work, as well as the gallery of work that is displayed in the classroom and other areas of the school. The repertoire of visual art work is enhanced through the school's collection of received art works, which provide the basis for the development of critical awareness as children view, discuss and write about items in the collection.

The visual arts repertoire, as for music, drama and dance, has the possibilities for diversity and should reflect a broad spectrum of activities and outcomes. The nature of art embraces a wide spectrum of experiences ranging from the abstract to pictorial and representational works. Pure forms of drawing, painting and modelling will either focus on outcomes that relate to the properties of the material or can be based on pure form and design, capturing thoughts and feelings in a subjective way. Representational art will include still-life, pictorial composition, puppets, masks, costumes, moving towards the production of artifacts that link with another subject area. The non-performing nature of art differentiates it from dance, music and drama in terms of the time aspect, but the rhythmic qualities of movement are captured through the rhythm of visual lines. The organisation of space is akin to choreographic understanding, and the organisation of pictorial content relates to dramatic understanding. Although individual art forms are uniquely different, there are some common elements and they share similar processes in terms of transforming an idea or feeling into an object of art or artifact.

The integrated arts approach engenders a wide variety of work and increases the arts repertoire of the primary school. By definition, an artifact can be a dance, a play, a musical piece, a painting. More specifically it could be a lyrical dance, a radio play, a percussion suite, a still-life painting. Pure forms can be compiled together to form an anthology based on a selected theme. Other forms such as the musical, dance drama, or puppet show are integrated products in their own right. Teaching is planned to follow linear pathways in each arts area which children follow as part of the National Curriculum programmes of study, with integrated arts workshops occurring towards the end of a cycle of learning, perhaps on a half-termly basis, or in units of four, five or six weeks' study, depending upon the age of the children. A main theme or topic, chosen as an arts project or relating to another subject area within the National Curriculum (for example, a science or history topic) will unify teaching and learning experiences. This is expressed in Figure 1.4 and shows the way in which National Curriculum attainment targets are met. The delivery of

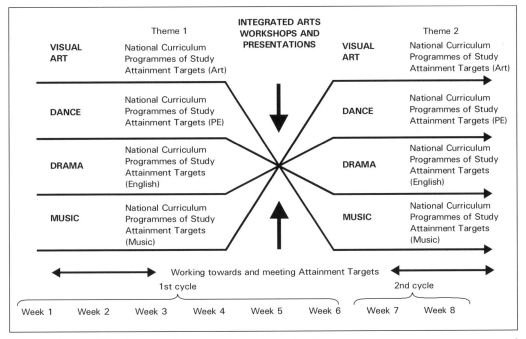

Figure 1.4 Teaching integrated arts – pathways showing links between dance, drama, music and art and the integrated workshop or presentation on a timescale of six weeks

lessons may be single-subject based or combined according the nature of the lesson and the relationship between subject areas. Figure 1.5 is a diagram drawn from the perspective of each major arts area, giving some indication of the varied and volatile relationships that can occur when the arts are integrated in pairs with one form providing the main teaching and learning focus. Each art area, according to the lesson being taught, becomes the main element of learning and is supported by another area. The major/minor role is determined by the focus and subject content of a lesson, which in turn is determined by prior learning and intended outcomes.

The integrated arts teaching programme comprises three main types of teaching sessions:

- single subject sessions in dance, drama, music or art
- integrated sessions, when two subjects are taught simultaneously within the one lesson, one of which will have the main focus
- integrated arts workshops which demonstrate the culmination of the particular teaching cycle incorporating each of the four areas.

Figure 1.5 A diagram showing main focus areas of dance, drama, music and art with combined art forms in teaching sessions

TEACHING METHODS AND APPROACHES

To achieve the best possible results when teaching integrated arts, it is highly recommended that a quick and efficient planning process should prepare the way. Documentation needs to be workable and exchangeable between colleagues so it should be informative, showing the main teaching aims and learning objectives in a succinct but meaningful manner and allowing for professional interpretation based on the teacher's understanding of the children's needs. There are four distinct stages:

- Stage 1 – identification of a theme followed by brainstorming of ideas put together by class teacher, class teacher and children, or class teachers and colleagues
- Stage 2 – preparation of medium-term programme over a period of four to six weeks
- Stage 3 – preparation of individual lesson plans, monitoring and evaluation of teaching sessions
- Stage 4 – recording and reporting progress as data for next cycle.

The overall amount of time to be spent on the programme needs to be determined in advance. For example, whether it will be running concurrently with other teaching and learning programmes of the National Curriculum over a period of four, five or six weeks.

Stage 1 needs to reflect all the ideas that come to mind arising from the chosen theme or stimulus. The starting off point can be a topic linking in with a programme of study in another curriculum area, it can be a free-standing arts based topic using an artistic stimulus, perhaps a piece of music or a painting. It can link to a visit or a special event. Write down ideas that come to mind based on the theme and organise them according to the subject areas of dance, drama, music and visual art (see Figure 1.6). This first stage represents the

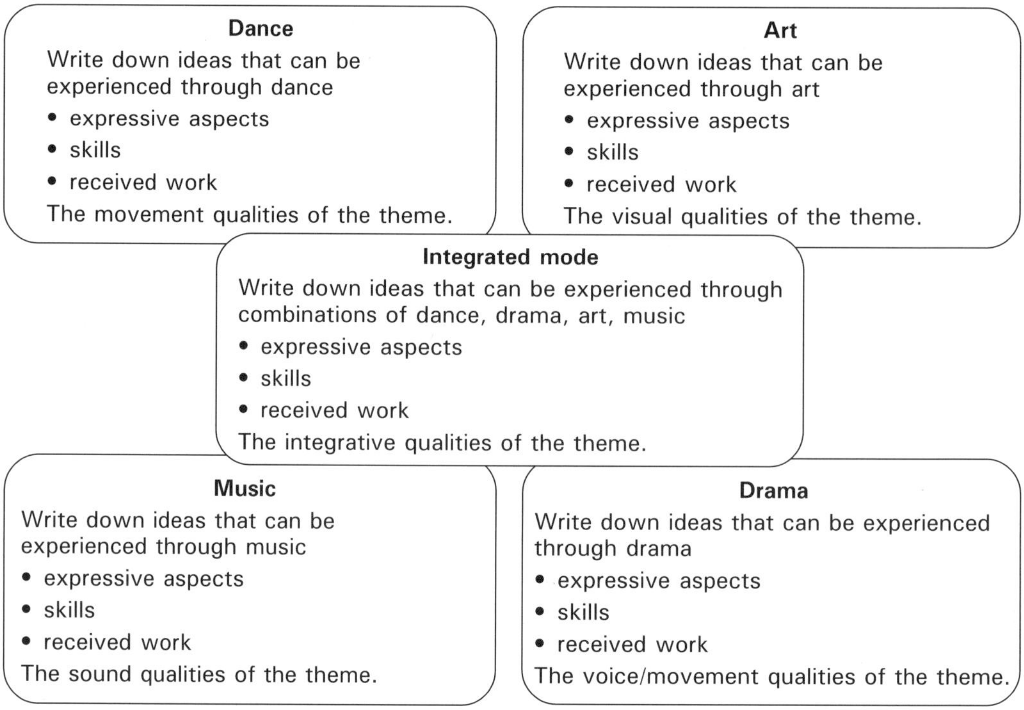

Dance
Write down ideas that can be experienced through dance
- expressive aspects
- skills
- received work
The movement qualities of the theme.

Art
Write down ideas that can be experienced through art
- expressive aspects
- skills
- received work
The visual qualities of the theme.

Integrated mode
Write down ideas that can be experienced through combinations of dance, drama, art, music
- expressive aspects
- skills
- received work
The integrative qualities of the theme.

Music
Write down ideas that can be experienced through music
- expressive aspects
- skills
- received work
The sound qualities of the theme.

Drama
Write down ideas that can be experienced through drama
- expressive aspects
- skills
- received work
The voice/movement qualities of the theme.

Figure 1.6   Stage 1 of planning an integrated arts programme for four weeks

ideas and information regarding the subject area which should be sought from reputable sources so that a quantity of reference materials can be compiled. In the first instance, materials that inform the teacher's understanding and in the second instance, utilising and collecting resources that the children can use. In this manner, a bank of information will be accumulated, reflecting the 'body of knowledge' in a particular field of study.

At this point, the teacher should envisage the intended outcomes and what type of experiences will need to be offered to the children for the outcomes to be achieved. Some ideas will be very clear while others may at first be diffuse and rather hazy, but this is part of the planning process – just as children need time to develop ideas so teachers also must have time to ponder on the journey that lies ahead. Children reach their destinations because their teachers devise the routes they will need to follow. The second stage of planning is the determination of the route, and this is where teaching skills and knowledge of the arts are applied. As thinking becomes more pronounced, the teaching and learning processes and the intended outcomes gain clarity.

Stage 2, recording the information for the medium-term planning, shows how the initial ideas have been sorted and categorised into the chronological order of teaching according to the arts subject area – visual art, dance, drama, music and integrated lessons. It provides an outline of the content of the sessions as they will be experienced sequentially. The content is structural rather than prescriptive and will be adaptable to circumstance (see Figure 1.7).

Stage 3 is the blueprint for an individual lesson, and expresses graphically the outline and content with clear aims, objectives and outcomes, revealing how the medium-term plans are applied according to units of time and learning. This may range from some very short lessons of about 15 minutes' duration based on an infant dramatisation or song, to intensive lessons of 45 minutes to one hour's duration with a Year 5 or 6 class studying visual art. Lesson plans ought not to be descriptive, but simply state the content of a lesson according to a learning framework, listing techniques, materials, items of equipment and other relevant resources as outlined in Figure 1.8.

A lesson plan is a blueprint, analogous with the architect's plan, but instead of being concretised in a building, it manifests itself in a taught lesson. Lessons themselves should be the masterpieces of professional artistry. They contain carefully thought out intentions and outcomes, and provide learning experiences in the arts which relate to the four main areas of participation, repertoire,

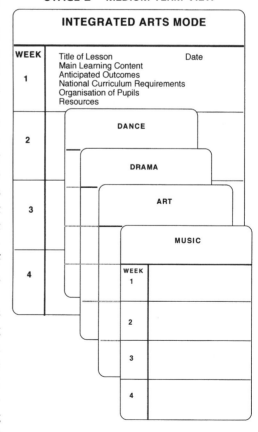

Figure 1.7 Stage 2 of planning an integrated arts programme for four weeks

STAGE 3 – LESSON VIEW

Title/aim:

Date:
Time:
Pupils/year group:
Numbers:
Venue:

Context: Where the lesson belongs in a series.

Focus – subject (S)
[Dance/drama/art/music/integrated arts]

Purpose:
 Concepts
 Knowledge
 Skills
 Attitudes

Creative thinking – forming ideas
 Presentation of the stimulus and forming ideas
 Explanation, demonstration and practice of techniques
 Interaction with pupils

Creative process – working through ideas
 1. Responding and experimenting
 2. Linking techniques with ideas
 3. Creative problem solving and solution seeking
 4. Shaping ideas into artistic forms related to theme
 5. Encouraging self-evaluation by pupil and enforcing maximum concentration on task

Creative communication – realising through ideas
 Completing the task – or reaching a stage of completion if the activity will carry over into another lesson

Critical response to the lesson
 Were the objectives achieved and the purpose met?
 Standard of response from individual pupils
 Teacher's role in developing the learning process
 Strategy for next lesson

Figure 1.8   Stage 3 of planning an integrated arts programme

understanding and context. Each lesson provides the planning information relating to:

- the aim, context and purpose of the lesson – identifying main concepts, knowledge, skills and attitudes
- the teaching strategies for encouraging creative thinking, creative processes and creative realisation (additional time may be required to complete work)
- the critical response, including the ways in which children discussed their work as well as the teacher's own self-evaluation of the effectiveness of the teaching methods.

Stage 4 is the record of the achievements of the children. Envisaging or ascertaining what the children will achieve as the culmination of an arts project determines the programme and progress of learning to reach the set target. Knowing what skills and techniques and modes of thinking are required shapes the content of each lesson en route. The teacher's analysis provides the children with the means of synthesising their own ideas – this is the way in which teachers facilitate children's creative growth. Monitoring children's progress is a continual process but a systematic recording of achievement is usually made on a termly basis. Figure 1.9 is a suggested format for a Record of Achievement report. Guidance in making judgements and evaluating children's progress in the arts is provided in Chapter 7 ('Professional Growth').

STAGE 4 - RECORD OF ACHIEVEMENT

INTEGRATED ARTS RECORD

Name of Pupil   **Year Group**

Levels of achievement in Dance/Drama/Art/Music
and Integrated Arts

	Formative Comment
CREATIVE PROCESS Pupil's response to art-making	
CREATIVE COMMUNICATION Nature of work produced	
CRITICAL UNDERSTANDING Pupil's response to own work and that of peers	
CONTEXTUAL UNDERSTANDING Discussion and writing about art works	

Summative Statement

Teacher's signature   **Summative Grade**

Date

Figure 1.9   Record of Achievement report

A WORKING EXEMPLAR

The following account of the Seascape Arts Project is a working exemplar or blueprint for learning that teachers are invited to interpret and adapt for use with their own classes. It demonstrates how, when the arts are taught and experienced in an interrelated manner, rich and varied teaching and learning opportunities result. The project can be adapted for all year groups in the primary school, but is broadly discussed in two parts, with ideas for Reception and Key Stage 1 followed by material suitable for Key Stage 2. A list of useful resources is included. All good teaching arouses the children's curiosity and maintains their interest, develops their skills, deepens their understanding and promotes independent thinking. The Seascape Arts Project exemplifies the processes of exploring, creating and appraising as reinforced through experiences in art, dance, drama and music, and demonstrates how one area of learning generates activities in another. It illustrates how the teacher can maintain a continuous momentum through the interaction of the National Curriculum attainment targets. For example, the appreciation of a received work in music (whether Saint-Saëns' 'Aquarium' from the *Carnival of the Animals* for a class at Key Stage 1, or Gustav Holst's 'Neptune' from the *The Planets* suite for a group at Key Stage 2) can be achieved through interpretation in movement which will stimulate creative work in dance. The choreographic structure of the dance will relate to the musical structure of the music. Endings can give rise to beginnings, whether in the same art form, or across the arts; frenzied activity can be interspersed with quiet contemplation, as children produce their own work, examine it and communicate their thoughts through discussion or writing. In visual art it might be that the teacher refers to how the painter Joaquin Sorolla y Bastida captures the warmth and pleasure of the seaside in the painting *Children on the Beach* (Museo Del Prado, Madrid) or, with older children, how the French impressionist Monet uses colour to capture the mood of the coast in the painting *La Plage de Trouville* (National Gallery, London). These experiences will not take place in isolation, but will be part of an interrelated experience that informs the children's own work in the arts project as a whole.

A group of infants sitting in a circle in the middle of the hall were presented with a variety of sea shells, fossils and *objets trouvées* from the sea-shore. They listened to the sound of the sea in the sea shell as it was passed around the class; they observed and felt the patterns and textures of the shells and through question and answer they found out about the habits and habitat of the sea creatures. This experience, which along with classroom displays and visual material, provided children with the necessary resources to conjure up images in their minds. The visualisation of the seascape based on what was seen and felt transferred itself into the movement session, when the children were taught how to use their body to make shapes based on the sea shells, stones and driftwood. The linear, rounded, or twisted shapes, with different points and patches of the body as weight-bearing parts nudged and tumbled, rolled and jostled into new resting places according to the imagined shift of body position as empowered by the sea. Similarly, the patterns of ripples, waves, bubbles and sea creatures were delineated through gestures of arms, or legs. The seascape, so encountered through the feel of movement, was enhanced through sounds made by the percussion instruments – the gentle rhythm of the tambour denoting the tidal beat, the rasping sound of pebbles thrown and rolled by the actions of the sea echoed with the gentle handling of a maracas. Experiments in shapes and patterns of movement are supported by, and in themselves support, the experiments of sound patterns. Either the teacher plays the instrument with all the children responding, or children work with a partner or in groups, so that the sense of sound and movement coexist. These experiences help children's understanding of the construction of movement and sound and prepare them to interpret recorded music.

The essential qualities of artistic creativity are supported by the beauty of the received work, which enhances the child's own experiences and provides a key to cultural understanding, especially when examples of music, paintings, poetry and stories of the sea can be drawn from a variety of sources from around the world. Scientific books and information relating to the shorelines, tidal movements and marine world will abound in the classroom. These are factual reference sources that help to fuel the visual imagery which forms the basis for creativity. The shells and objects that led to the dance, and the dance itself, provide inspiration for visual art work, musical composition and creative writing.

A collection of natural sea objects, nature's own artifacts, along with flotsam collected on a local coastal strip was arranged for a drawing lesson. Using choices of papers, pencil, charcoal, pastel or crayon, observational drawing took place, noting and recording such qualities as colour, texture, shape, shadow and highlight. This process of investigating excites the 'intelligent eye' and, with shrewd teaching, helps the child acquire the technical skills of handling and manipulating the mark-making tools. How can the marks of a pencil express the object before me? How can my drawing show the delicacy of the sea shell, the brightness of the spikes, the subtlety of the delicate pattern, the tracery of the sea fern? How do I hold my pencil? In any investigative stage the teaching is at its most powerful.

The investigative stage led to a productive stage with the clear objective of creating a three-dimensional seascape environment. A background was prepared of translucent drapes and netting upon which artifacts could be mounted or suspended. Working in groups the outline designs were made. Paper and paint were the main materials used, with embellishment details picked out in tissue paper, crêpe paper, cellophane, glitter paint, buttons, sequins, raffia, felt, fabric and pasta. The design and technical skills used related to the appropriate key stages and a variety of sea creatures – including fish, a whale and a dolphin – were created together with various forms of seaweed, sea fern and sea anemones. Figure 1.10 provides the overview of planning for the project and shows the main learning content for dance, art, music, drama and integrated areas. Parallel lessons in each subject, of various lengths run alongside integrated sessions as detailed in Figure 1.11 and one lesson, Creatures of the Sea, with a music and dance focus, is presented in detail in Figure 1.12.

The same theme, planned for older children at Key Stage 2 shows the expectancies of National Curriculum requirements through a more challenging content. Figure 1.13 provides information for the main learning in dance, art, music and drama as well as the integrated activities compiled as a sea anthology. The wheel diagram, Figure 1.14, should be read in conjunction with Figure 1.5 on p. 13, since it illustrates the dynamic interaction of the subject areas. Figures 1.15 to 1.18 are seascape images, showing two- and three-dimensional art work arising from observational sketches.

A central area of study for Years 5 and 6 is Shakespeare's play, *The Tempest*. William Shakespeare was a great playwright whose gifts are immortal. His poetic use of language and precision of text communicate both mood, imagery and meaning. His portrayal of characters, who interact within interesting plots, conveys attitudes and feelings that are

Dance
- Expressive – dance composition of a scene beneath the sea
- Techniques – movement qualities – sequences of shape and pattern – individual and partner work
- Received works – ballet *Ondine* – choreography, Ashton

Art
- Expressive – creating a mural of underwater scenes
- Techniques – observational drawings of sea objects – 3D sea creatures using paper and paints
- Received works – *Ride in a Rowing Boat*, Mary Cassatt – *Boulogne Sands*, Philip Wilson Steer

Integrated mode
- Expressive – an anthology of music, dance, drama and art based on a story compiled by the class
- Techniques – movement, voice, and music synthesised into a presentation

Music
- Expressive – creating a sound picture of underwater scenes
- Techniques – use of percussion instruments and voice
- Received works – action songs – music of the sea – *La Mer*, Debussy – *Carnival of the Animals*, Saint-Saëns

Drama
- Expressive – dramatisation of a story and/or a poem
- Techniques – recitation – solo voice and group responses – improvised drama – props and simple costume mime activities
- Received works – *The Little Mermaid*, Hans Christian Anderson – *The Fish Who Could Wish*, John Bush and Korky Paul

Figure 1.10   Overview of Seascape Project, Reception and Key Stage 1

seemingly ageless. Ideas from some of his works are appropriate for children in the primary school and, in particular, stories and song lyrics are inspirational if interpreted in a manner to which the children can relate and understand. A synopsis of the story of the play, told by the teacher, with some selected readings prepared by the children, are ways of introducing Shakespeare in class. In this example, a short extract from the play provides the inspiration for drama, whereas the song lyrics provide the source of visual imagery for movement and music.

Shakespeare's own idea for *The Tempest* was based on a historical occurrence of 1609 when a fleet of sailing ships left Plymouth, England for Virginia, America. A few weeks into the journey a storm arose and scattered the fleet. One vessel, *Sea-Venture*, carrying the newly appointed Governor of Virginia, ran ashore at Bermuda, and miraculously, the company escaped death and were able to live on the island before making their escape nearly a year later. News of the adventure and escape reached England in 1610. Shakespeare, obviously inspired by the events and the report of the conditions of the new colony, incorporated a number of issues into the play, which was performed before King James I in November, 1611.

The teaching of integrated arts in the primary school incorporates four interrelated component models for dance drama, music and visual art. Integrative teaching of the arts

---

INTEGRATED ARTS MODE

Week 1	Title:	**Water Play at the Seaside (Focus on Dance)**
	Learning:	Using elevation, travelling, jumping, gesture and stillness to express patterns on the sand, the ebb and flow of the sea, waves, and water patterns
	Outcomes:	Interpretation of rhythm to link movements leading to interpretation of poem 'There are Big Waves' by Eleanor Farjeon
	NC targets:	Dance aspects of a and c
	Organisation:	Whole class with individual and partner work
	Resources:	Pebbles, shells and sand, poem, percussion

Week 2	Title:	**Sounds of the Sea (Focus on Music)**
	Learning:	To create a scene beneath the sea, depicting creatures and plants in sound. Using percussion instruments to understand rhythm, timbre, mood, contrast for: caves and caverns; darting fish; giant whale; dancing octopus
	Outcomes:	A class composition with four musical sections
	NC targets:	Music
	Organisation:	Whole class with sub-groups
	Resource:	Maracas, tambour, chime bars, tubular chimes, etc.

Week 3	Title:	**Creatures of the Sea (Focus on Music/Dance)**
	Learning:	To create a scene beneath the sea, showing creatures and plants in dance, musical accompaniment. Use of artifacts
	Outcomes:	A class dance interpreting music and including shape, levels and different types of travelling movements
	NC targets:	Music, art and dance
	Organisation:	Whole class with individual, partner and group work
	Resources:	Recorded music and masks

Week 4	Title:	**Sea Anthology (Focus on Music/Dance/Drama/Art)**
	Learning:	To compile an anthology built up from previous experiences in art, dance, drama and music
	Outcomes:	Whole class presentation of story: 'Water Play at the Seaside'; musical picture and poem; 'Creatures of the Sea'.
	NC targets:	Music, art, dance, drama
	Organisation:	Whole class with individual, partner and group work
	Resources:	Percussion instruments, recorded music

Figure 1.11   Seascape Project medium-view, Reception and Key Stage 1

demands that teachers have a working knowledge of each separate subject area, since to bring the arts together children must acquire and build upon the technical and creative base of each area. The following four chapters provide teaching rationale for drama, dance, music and art respectively, showing how each subject model relates to the integrated arts model.

STAGE 3 – LESSON VIEW

Title/aim: Creatures of the Sea (Focus: Music/Dance)
Context: Lesson 4 in a scheme relating to the topic SEASCAPE

Purpose:

Concepts:	Understanding about the natural movement of sea creatures
Knowledge:	Composing a scene under the sea in dance and music
Skills:	Using dance skills as individuals, pairs, group, to create the dance based on recorded music. Pattern, shape, sequence
Attitudes:	Aesthetic and creative

Creative thinking – forming ideas
Travelling quickly, travelling slowly, changing direction
Using general space well
Sudden stopping
Slow rising and sinking
Sudden running and jumping, as if over waves
Slow curling and stretching
Relate to imagery and experience
Skills – darting, rolling, spinning, jumping, turning, twisting, floating, dragging
Matching sound and movement – percussion

Creative process – working through ideas
Class group as coral reef
Name sea creature (recall from class activity or discussion)
Analyse – shape, direction, level and quality of movement
Examples: fish – darting/gliding (shakers); crab – scurrying/curling and hiding, weight-bearing (block); serpents – twisting, bending, meandering – follow-the-leader in linear group formation (shakers); bubbles – spinning/turning, rising, rolling (triangle); seaweed – reaching out, balancing, twisting, floating (jingles); starfish – star shape, wide, travelling (shakers); octopus – reaching out with tentacles – group shape; sea horses – gliding or galloping movements (tambourine)
Use suggestions from the children, working on principle of analysis and synthesis

Creative communication – realising through ideas
Work through the above in an agreed order, including what to dance as an individual, with a partner, and in a group.
Music: 'Aquarium' from *Carnival of the Animals* (Saint-Saëns).
Starting and finishing positions as coral reef
Practise and perform to music

Critical response to the lesson
Were the objectives achieved and the purposes met?
Standard of response from individual pupils
Teacher's role in developing the learning process
Strategy for next lesson
Standard of response in each section

Figure 1.12   Seascape Project lesson view, Reception and Key Stage 1

Dance
- Expressive – shipwreck and underwater scene
- Techniques – effort/actions – time, weight, space, group activities – dance drama – characterisation
- Received works – *Lament of the Waves*, choreography Frederick Ashton

Art
- Expressive – creation of an underwater environment
- Techniques – observational drawings – 3D and mixed-media artifacts
- Received works – *In the Well of the Great Wave of Kanagawa*, Katsushika Hokusai

Integrated mode
- Expressive – compilation of a sea anthology – storm and shipwreck – sunken ship and underwater scene – 'Full Fathom Five Thy Father Lies' (Shakespeare, *The Tempest*)
- Techniques – voice – poetry, script, improvisation – music and dance composition – all group work – coordinating dance, drama and music to a single narrative for presentation

Music
- Expressive – sounds beneath the sea – characters and inhabitants, mythical figures
- Techniques – use of voice and percussion – tape-recording composed pieces
- Received works – *Peter Grimes*, Benjamin Britten

Drama
- Expressive – enacting shipwreck scene from *The Tempest*, William Shakespeare
- Techniques – voice and movement – mime of mariners
- Received works – *The Tempest*, William Shakespeare – sea verse and narrative poems

Figure 1.13 Overview of Seascape Project, Key Stage 2

Figure 1.14 Integrated relationships for the Seascape Project. The wheel diagram shows how dance, drama, music and visual art, however arranged, will have both a secondary and tertiary influence on each other within a thematic context.

Figure 1.15 Prototype seaweed designed and
constructed by a student teacher

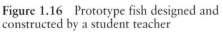

Figure 1.16 Prototype fish designed and
constructed by a student teacher

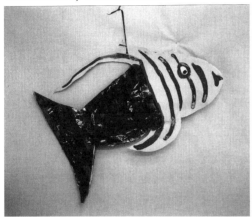

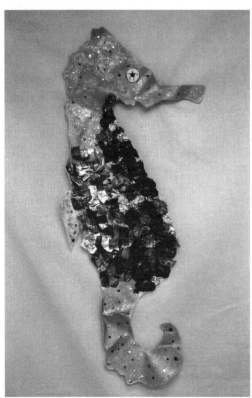

Figure 1.17 Prototype sea horse designed and
constructed by a student teacher

Figure 1.18 Prototype sea flowers designed
and constructed by a student teacher

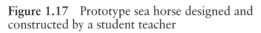

CHAPTER 2

The Drama Mode

Drama is one of the world's greatest art forms. It is a poetic art that presents images of life created through illusion. Its meaning is contained, conveyed and communicated through actions and dialogue that elicit a response from an audience, whose absorption in the symbolical portrayal of life is total. Drama, as performance, represents the passage of time. Events unfold through an air of expectancy and then out of the dramatic tension or conflict comes the resolution. Meaning in drama is comprehended through the interpretation of the thoughts, feelings, actions and interactions of the characters in a play, the *dramatis personae* around which the action is based. The performing area – perhaps a stage, an open air space, or, in terms of history, a Greek theatre, royal court, or medieval cathedral – are the physical arenas in which performances have taken place in the past and still do take place today. The combined forces of visual stage design, descriptive dialogue and the power of the imagination, creates the setting or location for the drama.

As an art form, drama utilises the human voice and sometimes musical instruments or electronic sounds for effect, reinforced through movement and visual design. These distinctive elements are juxtaposed according to the overall construction of the play. The role of the participants and the observers of the action build up a relationship which is based on the interpretation and understanding of both representational and symbolic action. Watching and understanding a play is rather like interpreting a painting, a ballet or a musical suite. It is a mental process associated with the sensory perceptions, a fully lived or aesthetic experience of engagement with the final outcome of a creative process that resorts to an expressive mode. What is comprehended is related to the knowledge and understanding of the onlooker, in terms of the constituent elements and the manner in which they provide an aesthetic and artistic whole.

Drama, as art, impacts into the contemporary world through traditional theatre, films, video and television and its influence on children, especially through the latest media forms, is profound. Children's first introduction to drama is rarely as the spectator-audience but more as the active participant. The youngest child learns about the world through enactment, whether the personal observation of domestic life or news events, and stories through play.

THE TEACHING AND LEARNING FRAMEWORK FOR DRAMA

As a component part of the overall teaching and learning framework for the integrated arts (as outlined in Chapter 1), drama teaching is based on the four major areas of participation, building up a repertoire, acquiring skills of critical analysis, and understanding the context of drama. This framework applies to the Reception class and pupils at Key Stages 1 and 2. It is constructed in a manner that provides children with a conceptual understanding of the major elements or aspects of drama arising out of their practical experiences with the National Curriculum 2000.

The major elements of drama teaching are based on the children's abilities in speaking and moving, improvising, composing, and performing. They incorporate and develop the children's skills of listening, looking, reading, and writing. Critical understanding is communicated through discussion or writing, using different media forms, and refers to the practical presentation, or performance mode of drama, from the stance of the child, either as participant – writing about personal experiences within a performance – or as a member of an audience. Children will enjoy reading published texts, chosen to reflect their key stage, but the substance of understanding the nature of drama in the primary school arises out of the performance mode, and in this respect, refers to the way in which the teacher and the children understand the performance.

Drama based on stories and songs is ideally suited to work at Reception and Key Stage 1 and is part of meeting the specific requirements of the National Curriculum 2000 which expects children to use language and actions as means of exploring and conveying situations, characters and emotions.

Drama commences from child play and progresses to structured play, games and singing games, onto play-making and performing before others, mostly peers in the same class. Children create and sustain different roles, either on their own or when playing with other children or adults. Lateral cohesion takes place as children are offered supportive experiences in each of the other three arts areas – music, dance and art. A framework for teaching and learning drama includes four aspects:

- participation in drama – children's practical knowledge of play-making through performance
- repertoire of drama – children's accumulative knowledge shown in the plays they can perform (invented or interpreted)
- critical skills of drama
- context of drama – children's knowledge of the historical, social and cultural worlds that have inspired or informed their own drama.

It is a requirement that children are able to comment constructively on drama they have either watched or in which they have taken part. A diagrammatic representation of this working theory is work shown as Figure 2.1.

PARTICIPATION IN DRAMA

Drama is accessible to all children – it is theirs by right of birth – from the moment of make-believe play, which can range from talking to themselves or an imaginary friend, of

Participation

Acquiring the techniques of drama:

- learning to act
- learning to invent
- learning to interpret
- learning to construct and write scenarios
- speaking and listening
- moving and observing
- interacting with others
- being and becoming through improvisation and characterisation
- practising and presenting

Repertoire

Acquiring a collection of dramatic experiences through:

- practising and rehearsing
- performing and presenting
- learning and recalling over the school year
- make-believe and play-making
- enacting stories and poems
- mime and puppet plays
- dance drama
- musical stories
- individual, group and class work

DRAMA

Context

Discovering about drama through:

- visits to the theatre, pantomime and festivals, television, radio and films
- books and stories about drama
- famous plays and famous playwrights
- working with drama in education groups

Critical awareness

Discussion and writing about the dramatic experience:

- as self-analysis
- as audience watching peer groups
- as audience to professional live drama
- as audience to film/video or radio/ sound play
- reading criticism
- developing a metalanguage to discuss the dramatic experience

Figure 2.1 A framework for the teaching and learning of drama

careering down the street, zooming around like a space rocket or aeroplane, engaging in conversation with dolls, or puppets and pretending to be someone else, perhaps hiding behind a mask, as depicted in Figure 2.2. It is by observing people around them, imitating their actions or mode of speech, pretending to be the characters in stories they have read or from television programmes and films they have seen, that children enter an inner world of practical realism or romantic fantasy. They process their ideas into images and invent scenes and snatches of drama that can be lone experiences or shared experiences with other children or adults. Indeed, adults can assist and encourage this development by providing costumes, toys and books that

Figure 2.2 Large puppets and mask designed and constructed by student teachers

facilitate learning through play. The early experiences of child play and fantasy are important in nurturing creative development and provide the foundation for drama in the primary school. They include social interaction, assimilation of experiences from the child's own world as well as the escape into the imagination, much of which is supported by stories, poems, pictures and other forms of exciting stimuli.

Speaking and listening skills are developed, and from role-play and improvised drama, a dialogue emerges, which, although spontaneous at first, after reshaping and re-enacting can be performed and shared by others. The story, incident or point of view assumes a dramatic form. The early stages of drama may have ideas based on a doll's tea party or a teddy-bear's picnic. The home corner is the obvious place for this type of activity, especially when it can so easily be transformed into other types of environment – perhaps a castle, a ship, a restaurant, animal hospital, a cave, hollow tree trunk, or even a giant fruit. The imaginative use of drapes, posters and children's own art work in the centre, along a wall, or in the corner of the classroom provides stimulating sets that can help to fuel the imagination. It is through such structured environmental play experiences, or creative play-making, that children first begin to acquire the techniques of drama. When more space is required and the drama lesson takes place in the hall, then the location or environment reasserts itself in the children's imagination, as the hall is transformed into a strange planet, a factory, and so forth. Fundamental to this is learning how to be inventive. This manifests itself in two ways – the invention of story-line and the invention of character – both of which provide inroads to acquiring improvisational skills through role-play.

Plots and characters emerge from play and become structured through repetition. Invention in drama is practical – a 'doing' experience that only comes alive through the act of performance – so closely linked to the ability to invent is the ability to act. Acting out a scene is closely related to the playing out of an idea which is the major characteristic of children's fantasy play. It is a playful and game-like experience. (In medieval times, the term *ludi*, meaning games or play, was the name for plays performed at court during Christmas which resembled mummers' plays with costumes and disguises. *Ludi* also included tournaments, sports, morris dancing and folk-games of the period.) The two major elements of drama required for acting out ideas are speech and movement, and the way in which these are correlated in order to express or substantiate a particular idea. The manner in which children react and interact together is vital, the experience of doing, thinking and feeling needs to be shaped into what can be termed dramatic form – a beginning, a development, a climax, an anti-climax and a resolution. Once this stage has been reached, the improvised drama can be recorded, either using a tape-recorder, video or written script. A transition takes place between the spontaneous response to a structured response that takes on form. The performance mode in drama enables children to be dramatists and actors since they act out their own ideas and create their own performance text or scenario.

Constructing and writing scenarios are an important aspect of drama at Key Stage 2 and can be approached in two ways. Firstly, recording the practical experience when the form of the drama has been shaped through group improvisation, or secondly, as a written project, produced by individual children, either independently, with partners or as a group. The organising principles for the drama can be based on a number of resources or suitable stimuli, for example, by examining some historical archive materials, reviewing a news event, an issue, or visit. As soon as a written script or scenario emerges, the next stage of putting the ideas into practice requires the ability to read the script and make it come alive through presentation. Drama may become the main focus in project or topic work, linking with science or history. In these instances it takes on a particularly valuable role as a vehicle for learning, not only enhancing other forms of cognitive learning but also drawing upon the children's knowledge base to inform the drama.

Constructing a scenario for drama means:

- stating the title of the play
- providing the background information giving details about the events that have led up to the present time
- stating the location and historical time of the play
- stating the *dramatis personae* – the characters in the play with a brief description of each one
- writing a story outline – beginning, middle and ending
- including key speeches, either for children to learn or around which to base their own improvised dialogue
- showing group voices and sound effects
- giving directions and/or descriptions for movement.

A scenario can grow out of improvised lessons, or may be constructed by the class teacher, or teacher and children together, and is a written response to the creative task of putting a play together.

A play script will provide greater detail of what each character says, and can be written by individuals or groups of children together. For example, children could write the script for a puppet play, either as a collaborative experience or with each child responsible for the lines of a particular puppet.

THE REPERTOIRE OF DRAMA

Over the course of the academic year each class will build up its own dramatic repertoire as part of the integrated arts mode. This class repertoire will reflect the nature of the work undertaken, and in addition to short remembered items, or drama games, will include work that has been crystallised from improvisational or script-writing workshops with photographic records of more ambitious presentations for school assembly, special occasions or end-of-term celebrations. The content of the drama will be based around stories, topics and poems studied and will often include other related arts areas. The class's repertoire will include work undertaken by individuals, partners and group activities, as well as whole-class involvement. The length of performance pieces will vary according to their nature and the level and ages of the children, but are likely to range from two or three minutes for solo, partner and small group activities presented a regular basis in class, to around 30 minutes for a well prepared and rehearsed performance for a special occasion – even then it is preferable for the performance to be subdivided into a number of shorter sections. The approach should be one of sharing, using a natural and accessible style of presentation that avoids entering into the realms of adult theatre.

The average drama repertoire as part of an integrated arts programme is likely to include Reception class and Key Stage 1 children knowing a selection of games, stories, poems and action songs, used as a means of acquiring voice and movement skills. At Key Stage 2, children in each class will have formulated short group presentations to peer groups, and one or two important works, perhaps of 20 to 30 minutes duration, created, practised and possibly presented before a school audience.

CRITICAL SKILLS OF DRAMA

Children develop their critical awareness in drama through writing about their own personal experiences, either in what they have done, or in what they have observed other children do. Acquiring the skills of observing drama means careful observation of movement, facial expression, and listening carefully to words, all of which are the clues by which children gain insight into understanding the characters in the play. Equally, capturing the atmosphere of a scene and the underlying meaning of action are ways that children are gripped by performance and get drawn into the action. Looking at a video, or a class criticism of a live presentation are valuable writing experiences, aided by reading criticism of dramatic productions often to be found in newspapers and journals.

Acquiring a critical language is known as the metalanguage (the language used to describe understanding of meaning in the arts), and is a valuable part of an arts education. The interpretation of dramatic experiences is based on a combination of the following stages:

- the skills of observing and understanding the visible presentation of drama including movement, interaction, facial expression
- the skills of listening to and understanding words
- the conjoining of these experiences
- the reading of play texts produced by themselves and others.

The two major forms of communication in drama are the spoken language and the gestural language which are united through performance. Learning about how to use the voice and how to move in drama are essential to this understanding, both in terms of how pupils can create their own works and how they can interpret, through listening and watching, the work of others. This will include being part of the audience for short playlets produced in class by peers, presentations by children in school, as well as the professional productions in the theatre, on television or in school by visiting companies of actors.

CONTEXTUAL AWARENESS OF DRAMA

The new millennium model for teaching integrated arts draws inspiration from the cultural heritage of drama as a means of enriching children's own creative and expressive experiences, not only by helping them to transform ideas into dramatic form but also by assisting them to comprehend how their own work fits into the wider arena of the received works. Teachers will make appropriate selections and references to the received works of drama as means of informing their own teaching and enhancing the children's understanding of the drama mode. Primary school children will gain their practical experiences of drama in the classroom, hall, playground, or special environment, perhaps a historical site. Building upon practical engagement at their own level, children will become inculcated into the cultural heritage of world drama especially if they are taken on visits to the theatre, or have professional artists to provide workshops in school. Films or videos suitable for children should be part of the school's art resource, along with books and stories about drama, and a selection of scripted plays for the older Key Stage 2 classes (Years 5 and 6).

VOICE AND SOUND

The poetical power of drama stems from the effective use of the voice when an empathetic and thoughtful delivery is able to capture the innermost meaning of the word. From the Reception class onwards children become sensitive to sound production and as teachers provide them with the means of gaining understanding and control of the speech-producing organs. This is fun and exciting and links with literacy development and literary understanding – the former through pronunciation of words, the latter through recitation of extracts from stories and poems. Musical understanding through singing songs helps children to use their voices in an eloquent and effective manner. Breath, note, tone and word suggest stages in voice production which are necessary for role-play, improvisation, story-telling, group responses and, for older children, script interpretation. Voice is used to communicate to others and in school there are many ways in which it will occur. It may be at an informal level when children are working either with partners or in a small class groups. It may be at a more formal level when children are presenting their work to others, perhaps within the classroom or school hall, or on the occasions when plays are performed in other locations.

Understanding the human voice commences with body carriage and the awareness of what happens when we breathe, and the application of this understanding applies to music as much as drama. Carefully controlled breathing patterns are required for speaking, singing and dancing, so the training in one area will help the other. Vocalisation or sound occurs as the outgoing breath interacts with the vibrating vocal cords creating the waves that pass through the resonator and are heard as sound. Breath is like a column of vibrating air acting on the resonators in order to acquire tone.[1]

Pitch is a mental conception that determines at what frequency the vocal cords need to vibrate in order to produce a required note. Tension of the vocal cords produces the high notes. Most primary school children because of their age and development have high-pitched voices, and this is one of the delightful and distinguishing characteristics of primary school drama and music. It follows that children playing the character parts of adults, ogres, monsters or giants will need to concentrate and practise to lower the pitch of their voices, not only to reflect the type of character, but to express the mood. This can occur when the teacher reads a story and the children recite a line, for example, in the *Three Billy Goats Gruff*. As it is the ear that controls the 'image' needed to produce the note, it is important that training in listening takes place so that children can become acquainted with and understand the use of pitch. Musical instruments, songs and singing games are very useful in this context.

---

1. Martin, S. and Darnley, D. (1996) *The Teaching Voice*. London: Whurr Publishers.

The resonators of sound are the nose, mouth, pharynx and sinuses, all of which are hollow chambers. Resonators make vocal sounds resound because through their function of making speech sounds they determine the tone of the voice. The note produced by the vocal cords when excited by the breath is given tone as it passes through the resonators, but only becomes a word when shaped or described by the speech organs – the mouth, lips, tongue, palate, or throat. The main divisions of speech sounds are vowels and consonants. A vowel sound has a free or uninterrupted passage through the mouth and is shaped by varying the positions of the tongue and lips. In contrast, a consonant as an element of speech is formed by the contact, or approximation of two speech organs, thereby resulting in the interruption of the sound. Sounds and words both contain and convey meaning. When children understand and control their speech the authenticity of meaning or mood is communicated more effectively.

Sensitive development of voice and listening skills takes place from infancy, beginning with the rhythmical rocking and singing, games, animal stories and sounds that growing children at first hear from members of the family or nursery. Active responses help to develop confidence, and materials and resources need to be selected to ensure progressive development of speaking and listening skills within dramatic contexts from the Reception class through the key stages of primary development. Learning off by heart from aural engagement, copying adults and other children, even as a collective chant, will eventually lead to reading out aloud together in the literacy hour. Children are empowered through the understanding of the function and beauty of language, and as the awareness of word sounds and language patterns are absorbed the auditory imagination is developed. Shaping words results in clear enunciation and pronunciation when children are taught to identify the sounds of vowels and consonants and the specific speech organs that are brought into use.

As vocalised breath passes through the mouth it makes a vowel sound, the quality of which is governed by the positioning of the speech organs, often the area of the tongue (front, middle or back) in relation to its position in the mouth, and the shape of the lips. There are pure vowel sounds which are produced when the speech organs are held in one position and diphthongs which are the sounds made when the speech organs move throughout the formation of the sound, known as a glide.

The position of the tongue, held steadily in the mouth, with a smooth flow of breath determines the quality of the pure vowel sound, as for example, in deed, seed, bead, reed, feed, lead, mead; free, did, bid, lid; dead, read, said, fed, bed, ted; dad, bad, fad, mad and lad, which are all sounds made with the front of the tongue. Vowel sounds using the back of the tongue are boot, shoot, root, toot; look, book, shook, rook; hawk, talk, balk; rock, choc, block; hut, nut, tut, and yard, lard, bard. There are nine diphthongs in the English language and each one is a created by a continuous glide of sound from one vowel position to another, as in near, here, bare, rare, hare, fair, boar, roar, pour, tour, may, say, fay, day, sigh, die, lie, rye, how, now, toy, boy, roy, toe, doe and foe.

Consonants depend upon the outgoing breath becoming impeded, usually through the use of the lips, nose, tongue or throat. Labial sounds such as P, B and M are produced through contact with the lips, whereas F and V are labio-dental sounds, produced by using the lips and the teeth. Lingua-dental sounds demand the use of the tongue and teeth – TH, DH, S and Z. The consonant sounds of L, N, T, D, R, SH, ZH, and Y are created through the use of the tongue and the palate, known as lingua-palatal, whereas the lingua-guttural sounds of G, K and NG use the tongue and throat. The sibilants or hissing consonants are S, SH, Z and ZH, the latter being voiced.

Young children delight in sitting in a circle making sound pictures based on the use of vowel and consonant sounds. Work of this nature, exploring sounds through making them and listening to them, provides valuable pre-reading experiences. The nasal consonants, M, N and NG can be used in turn to make a continuous melodic sound – mmmm; nnnn; ngngngng – but then to create a picture of droning voices and an atmosphere of calm, break the sounds into equal measures of four or six counts, with a clear break in between each note. A lateral consonant is the L sound, which again may be practised as a melodic line, rising and falling, getting louder or becoming softer, and then bringing in the word lullaby, as in the Shakespearian line, 'Lulla, lulla, lullaby; lulla, lulla, lullaby'.

Fricative consonants are the sounds TH, F, V, SH, H, R, and there is the rolled consonant sound, R, which can be repeated as 'r r r r' to make the sound of a snake or of a circular saw. To acquire sound awareness of the plosive consonants, P, B, T, D, K and G take each sound in turn and repeat it to a set rhythmical phrase, for example, 12 and 34, will become PP and PP, with emphasis on each beat in turn. Experimentation with voice tone and breath, changing of speed and strength will develop a greater sensitivity to voice sounds and their application in school. The same method and teaching style may apply to the affricate consonants of CH, G and J, building up to sound pictures of gurgling water, generators and jumping jacks. Make your own collection of evocative words that have interesting sounds and meaning; some may be action words.

1. Select a word and pronounce the word capturing its meaning.
2. Make up a sentence that includes the word.
3. Mime the sentence.
4. Read *Jabberwocky* by Lewis Carroll.
5. Use it as the stimulus for a sound study of voice and music either making a tape-recording to use as accompaniment to mime, or, working in groups, let the children learn one stanza and combine voice and movement.

Pictures, as visual stimuli, and later pictures and word cards to show graphic representation lead to the reading processes undertaken in literacy sessions. Start with all the children practising specific sounds varying rhythm, tempo speed, crescendo, diminuendo and silence selected according to the theme. Ensure correct delivery of sounds. Work out the narrative of the sound picture with the children, for example, a scene in the park on a summer's day could include insect sounds, children playing, a motor boat on the lake, birds singing, a dog barking – the wind starts blowing and the rainfall sends everyone scurrying home. Moving sound pictures suitable for a confined space when children each perform a mime action and add the sound are a further development, especially if made into a guessing game. Children can take turns to perform at the front or inside the circle, or all work together. Objects from the kitchen or bathroom, toy cupboard or story book are useful sources and there are many possibilities for example, a food mixer, a washing machine, or a fire-engine performed in groups.

Combining group sounds and actions is a development when the vocalisations – either sounds or words – act as accompaniment for mime actions. Objects and items explored at solo level can be used in group contexts, so that a small group can mime being on the bus, boat, or aeroplane, while another small group organise the sound. A scene from a story may entail one group of children in a mime activity, while others provide the sound background. A space rocket may be launched, the passenger train may leave the station platform, a factory machine is switched on. The sounds that are issued will be based on the understanding of their construction, both in terms of how the speech organs are used and how a sense of rhythm, tone, and projection occurs.

Sound pictures using the voice and utterances, as well as being linked with mime actions, can also lead to the use of words. Children can cope well at mixing sounds with words, and as they become familiar with the techniques that improve their articulation and projection – skills necessary for speaking in all contexts – they can incorporate the use of narration, poetry speaking and choral work. The use of onomatopoeia, when words are formed from sounds that resemble objects, can be used in drama and creative writing.

Knowing about the way in which words are formed and projected and the way in which they fit meaningfully into contexts is necessary both for creative and interpretative work in drama. Work on the voice should take place in an imaginative way on a regular basis. The time allocation for speech work will depend upon the age and experience of the children and the purpose of the lesson. Sometimes a whole drama speech session, lasting some 20 to 30 minutes, will be taught in conjunction with English writing and literacy. A combined session linking sounds with movement using hall time may also be of this duration. Shorter interspersions occurring at different points will draw from the repertoire built up over the year.

Sound impressions at Key Stage 2 can be recorded or presented as part of a radio play. Use as many different sound sources, non-verbal and verbal, percussion instruments and objects at hand to create sound pictures.

- Each sound picture will have a predetermined structure and content.
- It will contain a dramatic happening.
- The order – beginning, climax, anti-climax, resolution – should be clear.
- Children will work in groups and with individual parts.
- Use instruments and voice.
- Key words will shape the choice of dialogue.
- Expected length will be two to four minutes.
- Topics may incorporate the familiar and the exotic:

Tibetan monks chanting	a rainforest scene	wedding celebrations
a space station	a galleon/shipwreck	dockland scene
an alien invasion	a Victorian kitchen	a science laboratory
plague of Eyam/London	a highway robbery	a factory scene
a trade fair	a workshop	

Progress to scenes that incorporate movement and voice including issue based drama in which children act out social scenes. Allow children to offer contentious issues that have personal meaning and then progress to ideas and issues that require them to sympathise with another viewpoint. Whereas some approaches to drama lessons will concentrate on verbal communication, both as a training experience and creative output (for example, a play for voices to be recorded), other lessons will focus on movement – although most drama lessons will incorporate both movement and speech.

BODY AND MOVEMENT

Movement as a gestural language imbues drama with representational and symbolic meaning. The movement skills that primary children require in order to participate fully in drama range from natural, everyday actions and gestures to stylised, symbolical or representational movement. In the first instance, a child playing the part of a Victorian parlourmaid will need to carry a tray, set out cups and saucers and pour out cups of tea, either as mime activity or using real properties. These everyday movement skills will change according to the type of person the parlourmaid is, but if the maid is frightened, or feeling under suspicion, her everyday movement actions will also reflect this, so the child playing the part will show this. Understanding stylised and symbolical movements would be a prerequisite of a class enacting the story of the *Sleeping Beauty*, when slow rising and twisting movements, with percussion and narrative accompaniment, will depict the passing of 100 years. The castle becomes hidden away from the world, submerged in the clutches of a thick forest. The children's movements represent the dramatic context or environment. The manner of their movement will reflect the dark and menacing quality of the forest.

The spectrum of movement required within the drama mode ranges from the immediate and accessible actions and gestures of pure drama, through to mime and dramatic movement to dance drama, which is most akin to dance itself. Specific movement training in the primary school will take place within the context of both drama and dance lessons, in the same manner that voice training will take place in the context of both drama and music. The content and method will depend upon the focus of the lesson, but, through thoughtful planning there will be a transference of skills.

Children engaging in drama are acting out scenes. The nature of the movement is dependent upon the character being portrayed, the context of the characters in the play, and the events that happen including the time and place of action. It uses everyday actions and movements coloured by the characteristics of the part being played and the changing mood of the character as situations arise or viewpoints explored. Teachers encourage children to explore their own experiences of emotions and events in order to visualise what aspects to develop when acting out a particular scenario. The approach becomes more analytical as children progress through the primary years. Although first signs of acting out – including interacting with others, expressing a story-line, a character and a reaction to events – can be observed in young children playing and dressing up, the older children at Key Stage 2 are expected to think through character parts and events using ideas that are topical or linked with story work in English or appropriate studies in history, science or technology.

Mime is the art of communicating a story, mood, emotion, object or event without resorting to words. It expresses imaginative ideas by resorting to movement and facial expression as the principal modes of expression. Natural emotional expression (which convey how and why), and occupational gesture (depicting work and play) are the two aspects appropriate for children. Mime has an important role to play throughout the primary years, the study of which commences with nursery rhymes, songs, poems and stories of the Reception class. These develop into group mimes with a musical accompaniment, mimetic work actions and rhythms culminating with complex mime plays for older children. Short extracts of mime, with an accompanying or preceding spoken narrative, or music is a useful and effective approach. In addition to the popular fairground themes or clowning around, reference to literature is a valuable source and can encourage reading. For example, *The Outlanders*, by Helen Creswell contains a scene when the boy is confronted by wolves. A group presentation, with accompanying narrative and use of simple costume and masks, is a worthwhile and rewarding objective. Work dances and hunting scenes, using percussion, are ways of portraying myths and tribal legends and represent the transition from mimetic movement of drama and the ritual drama of dance in which animals, demons and gods abound. Figure 2.3 depicts masks and puppets based on legends from around the world.

The most important aspect of movement training for drama will take place in the dance lesson, which is currently placed within the physical education curriculum. Dance as an art form is based on an aesthetic and artistic codification of movement appropriate to the age ranges, the details of which are explained

Figure 2.3 Masks based on legends from around the world designed and made by student teachers

in Chapter 3, 'The Dance Mode'. Part of the programme of study for dance is the development of mood, feelings, attitudes and characterisations which are the essential elements of dance drama. The overlap between drama and dance is important and mutually beneficial and hall based lessons will provide movement experiences for children that can focus either on drama or dance, or combinations of the two as in the enactment of a dance drama, mime play or a scenario that combines the two.

Children's understanding of the nature of dramatic movement is based on the artistic skills they acquire that enables them to use their body in particular ways. It is based on the following key areas:

- characterisation – how a particular character moves
- mood – how movement reflects the change of emotion and state of mind of a character, or of self
- environment – how the setting for the drama can be depicted through movement, *tableau vivant* and statuesque.

Drama for the young is approached from the perspective of the natural and everyday experiences of movement, but also incorporate the stylised and exaggerated traits of characters from story, their facial expression and tone of voice matching that of movement when voice and movement come together.

Drama lessons taken in the hall commence with body awareness themes – stretching into a variety of shapes, changing muscular contraction to relaxation, awakening specific limbs of the body, and including stance and posture – so that the mental concentration on the dramatic ideas of the lesson become sharpened. There should be contrast between movements that are performed in place, and those that travel around the room, as well as including contrast of muscular tension and speed and direction of movements. Every lesson is unified by its theme and purpose, and the illustrative content demonstrating unity rather than being a collection of disparate activities. When planning a lesson, envisage the intended outcome and analyse its intended content from the perspective of the technique required. This information will provide the substance of the main teaching part of a lesson providing the children with the technical means of expressing creative ideas.

Human movement has four constituent elements or qualities which relate to the passage of time required to execute movement. These are:

- rhythmical qualities indicating fast and slow and gradations between extremes, including contrasting and gradual transitions
- dynamics of action indicating muscle tone and physical strength levels, from weak or gentle to tough and strong
- directions indicating the use of the spatial area, around the body and in the hall. Direct actions of limbs or striding out determinedly contrasting with circuitous pathways
- sense of flow indicating an overall characteristic of movement, ranging from that which is smoothly coordinated and flowing to that which is staccato and disjointed.

Speed in movement can be used in character portrayal. The quick movements of the mice in the *Pied Piper of Hamelin*, or the slow movements of the Selfish Giant in the Oscar Wilde fairy story, *The Selfish Giant*. As characters change mood, the speed of their actions will change, from the slow movements of sadness, fatigue or despair, to the quick movements of excitement, optimism, or anger. Dynamics of movement help to convey the character being portrayed. The strong movements of the Iron Man, when Ted Hughes's story *The Iron Man* is dramatised, or the gentle movements of Shakespeare's Titania, contrasting with the plodding movements of Nick Bottom and the fairy light movements of Puck, all characters from *A Midsummer Night's Dream*. Direction of movements help to convey the determination of an action, from decisiveness to uncertainty, from volatile darting and settling, to devious meandering. The overall sense of flow draws the other factors together and helps to focus on a particular character. Character portrayal in improvised drama and scenarios based on stories will often start with the exaggerated, larger-than-life parts. Preparation for play-making will require a movement analysis of each character based on the four essential elements of motion. Making statues, bringing in facial expression and making the statue come alive is a viable starting point. Working on individual tasks within the class, create a movement sequence based on a particular incident in the play. Devise partner work activities along the same principles, and then add dialogue, so that movement and voice become conjoined.

The factors of movement, as conceptual elements as well as being a working tool of analysis for the teacher, become powerful mechanisms through which the children can synthesise their ideas to form short character portrayals. The approach for characters can also be used for group work. In the same manner that in ancient drama the Greek chorus related points of action and change of circumstance, the use of coordinated actions suggesting changes of scene can be utilised. For example, from a group of individual children arranged proudly and well spaced, slow sinking and twisting movements leading

Figure 2.4   Using body shapes
to create an environment

to a group shape of contorted decay will convey the sense of foreboding, destruction and dying, perhaps related to the destruction of the environment from disease, war, or pestilence. Figure 2.4 shows how body shapes are used to create an environment.

THE PIVOTAL ROLE OF DRAMA

The distinguishing characteristic of drama is the performance mode, uniting voice and gesture through which the core of dramatic experiences can be expressed, interpreted and understood. The drama core segment as depicted in Figure 2.5 is dedicated to focused play activities at Reception and Year 1, leading to improvised drama at Years 2 to 6. Issue based drama, introduced at Key Stage 2, will utilise improvisational techniques and role-play. The dramatic narrative as identified in myths, legends, fables and tales is appropriate through all age ranges, while the historical narrative is more appropriate at Key Stage 2. The development of voice, the interpretation of play scripts and scenarios, documentary drama, and the selective use of poetry and prose complete the core drama cycle. Programmes incorporating these approaches are suitable through the age ranges, since it is the choice of materials and methods of approach that will be personalised to meet the needs of particular classes.

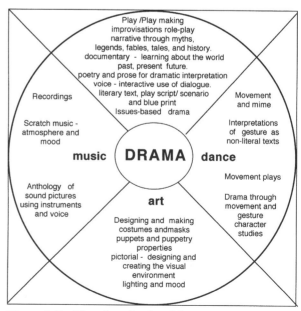

Figure 2.5   The pivotal role of drama

Specific links with art, music and dance emphasise the crucial role of drama within an integrated arts programme. In terms of music, scratch compositions by the children can be used effectively to provide atmosphere for drama, matching the mood of action and text. Links with art can be applied, not only through the costumes, masks, puppets or properties which can be used in the manner of applied art, but through the use of screens, wall displays and hangings constructed as settings. Large cardboard boxes painted with interesting designs and corrugated card can be used effectively as environments for drama in the classroom, corridor or hall, as scenery or puppet theatre, as illustrated in Figure 2.6. Movement skills in drama can be acquired in the dance lesson through understanding the significance of mime and gesture in character studies, through simple movement plays at Reception level to the rehearsed and refined presentations at Year 6.

Figure 2.6   Using boxes as sets for a puppet play

INTERPRETATION AND CONSTRUCTION OF TEXTS

The drama mode offers a wide range of interpretative experiences for children based on the making and acting out of short plays or anthologies of voice and movement. At primary school level, a dramatic work can exist in two ways: the written text and the performed work.

The written text is a representation of a performed work and may be a detailed published text specially written for children, an overview scenario put together by the teacher or children, or a play script written by the children themselves. Each of these examples could be termed the blueprint for performance since the words and instructions can be interpreted and brought to life through performance in school. In this instance, rather like a musical score, it is a starting point for performance. In contrast, a play script or scenario can be produced as a record of work that was created through the performance mode, so it becomes a written record of a drama experience that started with performance.

A play script is a literary form and requires skills of reading and writing. The use of new technologies is a viable form for producing play scripts. The full spectrum of experience in drama includes the interpretation of texts and the construction and reconstruction of the children's own works and that of others. The performance mode of drama is the living text, and the skills required in the process of creation, presentation and interpretation are those that are acquired in practical drama lessons aided by those in dance and music.

Early experiences of drama with Reception and Key Stage 1 children will usually focus on improvisational types of play and game activities, and will exist in performance mode only. It is more generally expected that the written text and performance modes will coexist with experienced classes at Key Stage 2 with children at Years 4, 5 and 6. Preparing and presenting a text infers operating in the performance mode, but does not presuppose that the finished version or production will be performed following a theatrical convention. Productions of drama, as in dance and music, are very likely to be short presentations of work to peer groups within the class, other classes within the school, and as part of school assemblies or the occasional special event. This type of production is the likely outcome of a series of drama workshops over a period of a few weeks.

Written texts can be formulated by teachers, or teachers and children, and can be based on a written scenario which indicates the characters in the play, the main plot and setting for the play. It will be a framework in which there is scope for improvisation set around selected key sentences. The following scenario is based on a drama workshop with a class of Year 4/5 children which took place as part of a visit to a heritage site. The children's main history topic was the Tudor period, and so a fictional scenario was created based on historical sources connected with the particular heritage site, which had an extensive family history connected with this period. It was written with a special focus on one of the children who lived in the house over 400 years ago who, at the time, would have been of the same age as the visiting class.

Learning about the Tudor period through the drama and related arts can be based upon the concept of a play within a play, with children taking on the roles of a family being visited by travelling players. Many people had heard about a new playwright called William Shakespeare who had been working for the Lord Chamberlain's men at the Theatre in London in 1594 prior to the opening of the famous Globe Theatre in 1599. Rich families often hosted players, dancers and musicians, many of whom roamed the country. The scenario for *A Midsummer Night's Dream*, as presented, shows the dramatic structure that was followed during a drama workshop in which the children provided their own musical accompaniment using percussion instruments. At the end, many performed a lively Elizabethan dance to a recording of music by Michael Praetorious (1571–1621). Solo voices, narration, improvisation techniques, reading and dancing all took part. Use of masks and costume highlighted the experience.

A scenario based on William Shakespeare's *A Midsummer Night's Dream*

A messenger announces the arrival of the players and musicians. Everyone begins rehearsing in order to perform a scene based on a performance given by the Lord Chamberlain's men in the theatre in London, in 1597. The characters in the play are:

Oberon, the king	Titania, the queen of the fairies
Puck or Robin Goodfellow	Fairies – Pease-blossom, Cobweb, Moth, Mustard Seed
Nick Bottom, a weaver	Other fairies and attendants

The children create the enchanted wood and set the scene as fairies, as other night creatures dart through the trees. They sit, spaced out in the performing area. Oberon and Titania enter with their train of followers making plans for midnight revels. They are quarrelling over the possession of the changeling boy who is attending Titania. Oberon wants the boy as his page, but Titania says:

Set your heart at rest, your whole fairy kingdom buys not the boy of me.

Oberon is cross and says before the morning dawn he will torment her for this. He then calls for Puck, his chief and favourite, and privy councillor who is a shrewd, knavish sprite, very mischievous and full of pranks. Oberon calls Puck over.

Puck. Fetch me the flower which maids call Love in Idleness. The juice of that little purple flower laid on the eyelids of those who sleep will make them, when they awake, dote on the first thing they see. Some of the juice of that flower I will drop on the eyelids of my Titania when she is asleep, and the first thing she looks upon when she opens her eyes she will fall in love with, even though it be a lion or a bear, a meddling monkey or a busy ape; and before I will take this charm from off her sight, which I can do with another charm I know of, I will make her give me that boy to be my page.

Puck dances off to collect the flower. Oberon goes to Titania's bower, a bank of beautiful plants including wild thyme, cowslips, and sweet violets, all growing under a canopy of woodbine, musk-roses, and eglantine. As the fairies sing her to sleep, the children re-form to create the forest and move, wearing masks they have made, as the creatures described in the song lyric.

You spotted snakes with double tongue
Thorny hedgehogs, be not seen;
Newts and blind-worms, do no wrong,
Come not near our fairy queen.
Philomel, with melody,
Sing in your sweet lullaby,
Lulla, lulla, lullaby; lulla, lulla, lullaby:
Never harm,
Nor spell nor charm,
Come our lovely lady nigh;
So good night with lullaby.

Titania is drowsy and as she is lulled to sleep the fairies creep away. Left alone, Oberon quietly comes towards Titania and drops some of the love-juice on her eyelids, saying:

What thou seest when thou dost wake,
Do it for they true-love take.

Children re-form as a group representing a different part of the forest where Nick Bottom the weaver has lost his way. He moves around aimlessly, but being tired he lies down and falls asleep. Oberon sees him and claps an ass's head over the clown's, scheming to play a trick on Titania. Oberon says:

This fellow shall be my Titania's true-love.

Bottom wakes up and cannot understand where he is. He goes across to where the fairy queen is sleeping. She awakens and speaks.

Ah, what angel is that I see? Are you as wise as you are beautiful?

Fairies come and attend upon the queen and the ass-headed clown. Oberon comes closer to the scene and reproaches her because she has lavished attention on the ass. Titania cannot deny this, and so Oberon carries on teasing her further until she relents and hands over the changeling boy. Oberon takes pity because he has had enough fun, so he throws the juice of another flower into Titania's eyes and as she recovers her senses she begins to wonder why she doted on the ass-headed clown. Titania then said she loathed the strange monster. Oberon takes the ass's head off the clown and leaves him to finish his nap. Oberon and Titania are now reconciled.

The play concludes with sports, revels and dances throughout the fairy kingdom. Players and company all celebrate.[2]

Teachers can select appropriate passages from Shakespeare and devise their own scenarios along the format of the above exemplar. It is important to capture the spontaneous aspects of child drama by avoiding unnecessary theatricality, and using informal performance areas. On the occasions when the work is shared with an audience, place chairs around the periphery. Published play scripts specially written for primary school children are also available and are included in the list of resources (see the Appendix).

UNDERSTANDING THE PROCESS AND RESPONDING TO THE PERFORMANCE

There is always a clear link between the process of learning about drama and the presentation of work to others. Teachers and children alike need to be mindful of this link otherwise the harmony of teaching and learning in and through drama will suffer. The reaffirmation of the drama mode as part of the integrated arts programme requires a clear understanding of what the teaching objectives and outcomes are. In all art areas, the teacher envisages the aspirations of the class and works towards these goals. By examining the intended outcome in terms of content, the teacher will ask what the children will need to know in order to make the idea a reality. In an integrated arts presentation that incorporates drama it will be necessary to draw up a medium-term teaching plan that provides the children with the means of making the drama work.

Realisation of goals, as established in planning exemplars presented in Chapter 1, is based on a teaching method that follows a system of analysis and synthesis. By making a careful skills analysis of the intended performance, it is possible to use this information to construct a series of medium-term plans followed by the individual lesson plans that provide a learning framework. Children will respond by building upon their existing skills and developing their artistry, both of which come together in the final presentation. The system of building up or synthesising ideas in this manner allows creative expression to lie at the heart of drama in the primary school. It enables children to progress by a series of problem-solving and solution-seeking processes, which by nature are linked to the final result. The process and the product are interrelated. This comes about through:

---

2. Shakespeare, W. (1596) *A Midsummer Night's Dream*. London: Spring Books.

- Purposeful and realistic planning that determines clear aims and objectives in drama at each phase – overview, medium term and lesson view.
- Purposeful implementation of concepts, knowledge, skills and attitudes through inter-action between teacher and pupils as part of an ongoing process during each drama lesson.
- Purposeful response and critical analysis of various aspects of dramatic engagement as an ongoing process during each drama lesson. This is a way of monitoring progress as part of continuing and summative assessment of children's creative ideas in drama. It occurs when working out ideas in an imaginative way but also when the ideas reach a performance level.
- Monitoring the standards of individual responses in drama.

THE TRADITION OF DRAMA AND THE CHILD'S CREATIVE SELF

From time immemorial, in most societies throughout the world children have grown up surrounded by the arts. Drama spectacle, whether as celebrations, rituals, forms of worship, or ways of enacting tribal histories often included children either as celebrants or spectators. One interesting example is the story of Nambaree, the six-year-old Aboriginal boy and a key figure in the life of the early colony, who observed the first fleet as it sailed into Sydney harbour in 1788. Journals kept by the early settlers provide an account of the drama surrounding Nambaree's initiation into manhood ceremony. There are many great histories of people which have been captured and communicated through drama. Most follow the oral tradition, many including solo voices, group chants or chorus, and include movement, use masks and have musicians. The folk-tales and legends and numerous creation stories are fertile sources for children's drama since they stimulate the imagination and provide great scope for interpretation using the method suggested. Children are the key players being other people, becoming more aware, and learning about the world through the stages and processes of drama that culminate in presentation.

RECORDING AND REPORTING OF DRAMA WITH CHILDREN

The final stage of teaching drama relates to self-evaluation based on intention, outcome and standard of work produced, set in the context and belief that the teacher does the utmost to encourage maximum response from the pupils, and that assessment of pupils' work is applied sensitively in a positive manner. This is based on educational judgements linked to set criteria as suggested in the previous chapter. Teachers establish and develop a particular approach which is based on their relationships with the children allied to their understanding of what they know and understand about drama. In terms of specific lessons, it is important to question how well each part of it went and how the intention matched the abilities of the pupils.

What should teachers look for in the evaluation of children's drama? The two most important things are the way the children conducted themselves in the lesson and the standard of work produced. Teachers must be aware of the manner in which the children engaged in the activity, the progress made through doing and discussing the drama text, as well as the end result. Did the children engage successfully in their work? How independent were they in the ways in which they concentrated? The important aspects to note are:

- the children's operational skills of play-making
- the children's achievements in production and presentation of drama
- the children's critical understanding of the operational process of drama including discussing and writing about drama
- the children's understanding of the cultural aspects of drama.

The type of observation, interaction, clarity of aims and objectives as outlined above necessitate an ongoing assessment process. Children's progress can be recorded at intervals as required by the school, based on observational notes relating to work within each project undertaken and consolidated each term. The kind of questions, the manner of intervention, the nature of the discussion all provide the means of extending the quality of both teaching and learning. These aspects are further developed in Chapter 7 ('Professional Growth').

CHAPTER 3

The Dance Mode

Dance as an art is totally reliant upon movement. To engage in the experiences of the dance, whether as a creator, performer, spectator or teacher, not only requires an understanding of the artistic and aesthetic nature of the organisation of movement but also a belief in its significance as a gestural language. Dance, as a major art form, uses the body to express metaphor and symbol through the formulation and organisation of movement patterns that capture and convey meaning. Evidence of dance, whether as art or social conventions, abounds since the world is a treasure store of dances of many styles, all of which have relevance to the people who have inherited or created them. Each major continent of the world reveals its own dances, most of which relate directly to cultural groups so that the spectrum of experience provided by dance in contemporary society is vast, and ranges from the fervour of disco dances and the practical immediacy of folk dances, to the sophistication of ballroom dancing and the highest technical and artistic demands of contemporary and classical dance styles.

Touring companies, world travel, films and video have brought dance from the inaccessible terrains of distant lands into the lives of many people. Britain, as a pluralist society, comprises peoples who have brought their dances with them such as regional dances of Europe, Afro-Caribbean islands and India. Solo dances, dance duos, group dances and large-scale displays typify the ways of organising dances for presentations, performances and grand spectacles.

Children's first introduction to dance in western society is through singing games and spontaneous rhythmical play actions, acquired through family, nursery and media resources. To dance is to move and childhood and movement are synonymous terms, for movement is one of the major characteristics and functions of life itself – without movement there is no life. Childhood is the vibrant growth stage of life that is full of exuberance and discovery. Healthy physical growth of children facilitated through dance includes intellectual, emotional and social development. The child's body is an ensemble of vital powers and the primal condition or orientational centre of how s/he perceives the world around him/her. It follows that dance programmes in school require the stimulation of children's consciousness of themselves, of being alive and of perceiving and understanding the world around them. Dance is experienced through awareness of kinaesthetic flow patterns, the awakening and development of skills through control, coordination and, above all, through significance and meaning of movement in a creative and expressive way.

The experience that teachers offer children leads to an understanding of dance as an artistic form, implying an awakening of movement in a symbol form in contrast to other forms of physical education. Dance education at Reception and Key Stage 1 provides children with an artistic language of actions which, linked with their intellectual and physical growth, is transformed into a significant and meaningful mode of communication.

THE TEACHING AND LEARNING FRAMEWORK FOR DANCE

The types and styles of dance taught in schools meet the needs of all children and are based on movement principles that all teachers understand and can teach. Teaching dance as part of an integrated arts model for the new millennium develops previous systems by incorporating the artistic, aesthetic, critical and cultural aspects of dance, which are provided as a coherent and developmental programme from Reception classes to Year 6.[1] The programme is enhanced by parallel and integrated studies in drama, music and visual art. Areas of study for children include:

- participation in dance – children's practical knowledge of dance through performance
- repertoire of dance – children's accumulative knowledge shown in dances they can perform
- critical skills of dance – children's knowledge of the qualities and special nature of dance experienced through participating and observing dance and expressed through discussion and writing
- context of dance – children's knowledge of the historical, social, and cultural worlds that have inspired or informed their understanding of dance.

Figure 3.1 exemplifies this working theory and includes key issues for each area of knowledge.

PARTICIPATION IN DANCE

Children's practical knowledge of dance through participation is based on their dual roles as creators and performers. Working out ideas creatively in dance means that children are putting ideas and feelings into a recognisable artistic form. The process stems from the natural, spontaneous movement actions of children, such as running, turning, leaping, jumping, curling and stretching. The body, as the instrument through which movement is expressed, is trained to perform the types of movement required to express a certain idea or to convey a particular mood. Analogous with speech, which is organised into the recognisable sounds and words of language, dance also has a semantic structure which provides the basis of how children can think and express ideas through movement. The

1. The codification and technique for movement and dance as introduced into British maintained schools is based on the system devised by Rudolf Laban (1879–1958) first published as a series of movement themes, Laban, R. (1948) *Modern Educational Dance*. London: Macdonald and Evans.

Participation	Repertoire
Participation Acquiring the techniques: • actions of the whole body – travelling, leaping, landing, jumping, turning, balancing • actions of specific limbs and head • coordinating movements • inventing movements • remembering movements • inventing dance • performing own dances and set dances • presenting dances	**Repertoire** Acquiring a collection of dances: • through practising and rehearsing, performing and presenting, learning and recalling over the school year • lyrical dance • stories in dance • dance in drama • social dances • individual, group and class

DANCE

Context	Critical awareness
Context Discovering about dance: • visits to dance performances, pantomime, festivals and television • books and stories about dance • famous ballets and famous choreographers and dance companies, local, national and international • working with community dance artists in education	**Critical awareness** Discussion and writing about the experiences of dance: • as self-analysis • as audience watching • peer groups in dance lessons and in school • as audience to professional companies • as audience to film and video • Internet • reading criticism – developing a metalanguage to discuss the experiences of dance

Figure 3.1   A framework for the teaching and learning of dance

dance skills that children learn are based on the conceptual understanding and perform-ance of natural actions, gestures and steps determined by spatial, dynamic and rhythmical structures. Figure 3.2 shows the movements of children captured at the moment of gently rising and extending, as they experience lightness and fine touch qualities.

Figure 3.2   A study of children showing their conceptual understanding and sensitive awareness of dance

Practical dance skills provide the movement language for creative thinking and forming ideas, and also prepare the body for the execution of movement. To attain their best personal aesthetic and artistic standard children must acquire body discipline and management. This means regularly practising in order to improve personal standards – maintaining balance, landing correctly and safely after a leap or jump. Every part of their body comes alive through the accomplishment of personal movement. Practical dance skills will develop children's strength correctly when each successive lesson provides a fresh and further challenge. Fitness can be maintained and children will develop efficiency of movement.

The National Curriculum requirements expect children at Key Stage 1 to use movement imaginatively as they develop control, coordination, balance, poise and elevation in the basic actions of travelling, jumping, turning, gesture and stillness. They are also expected to explore moods and feelings and to develop their responses to music through dance by using rhythmic responses and contrasts of speed, shape, direction and level. Children can also perform movements and patterns of movement, including those from existing dance traditions.

By the time Key Stage 2 is reached children are more sophisticated in the way in which they create and perform dances using a variety of movement patterns to express feelings, moods and ideas. They are able to respond to music and to create simple characters and narratives in response to a range of stimuli. They are also required to perform a number of dance forms from different times and places.

Children as dancers learn to interact with each other, whether as partners or in group dances which they have choreographed, or when they perform country, folk or ballroom dances appropriate to their age and ability. In this manner, they advance their personal and social development.

THE REPERTOIRE OF DANCE

Over the school year, each class will work towards building its own repertoire of dances which have been created, learned through practice and presented to the rest of the class or to a small audience. As the children improve body management skills, the level and quality of performance of finished dances will reflect an improvement in standards. Each dance will help to advance the children's abilities in composing and performing, and will continue to reflect their artistic growth. Children can be encouraged to rework their own choreography, or exchange their roles within a dance, especially where group or partner dances are concerned.

Children's dances reflect their level of ability in:

• the technical ability of performance, revealing the quality of expression and aesthetic attitude towards movement
• the level of creative understanding contained within the movement and its power to communicate – this will range from a complex and technically challenging content to one of greater simplicity, according to the age and aptitude of the children
• the children's ability to perform dances of different genres, such as: pure dance form, lyrical dances, dance drama, masked dance, anthologies of dance and other arts, and traditional dance forms.

Pure dance, as the name indicates, refers to dances that are conceived and arise exclusively from the rhythmic, spatial and dynamic structures of movement. They are abstract in nature and the children's understanding of them is based on their own ability to master the way they move according to the laws of motion and the elements of dance.

The choreography of pure dance provides the foundation of all dance experience, especially as each dance has a special focus related to at least one motion factor, whether the focus is on the whole body or specific parts of the body. Setting a task about the time factor would result in a rhythmical study. Using patterns created by arms and legs and linked with shape would indicate the use of the space factor, whereas making the body change its muscular tension or contraction would result in dances displaying a strong sense of movement dynamics. The time factor linked with the muscular drive expresses rhythm, whereas the spatial factor, linked with rhythm provides visual design. Isolating motion factors and concentrating upon creating sequences and short dance studies is the most effective way of discovering the power of dance and developing kinaethestic intelligence – the intelligence of movement. Children's dance sequences can be based on suggestions of structural content provided by the teacher and developed as improvisational responses to a particular piece of recorded music.

Lyrical dances are a development of the pure dance since the construction and content of the dance is organised to express a deeply felt emotion. If children create a dance of happiness, they will use the quick, light, elevated movements of joy, but if their dance turns to anger and aggression, the movement indicators will be strong and fast with earth-bound as well as elevational movements. Set tasks, perhaps working with partners and using percussion instruments as accompaniment to show contrasting emotions or feelings, will lead to a number of short studies in which mood and idea are captured in dance. An example could be a group composition showing: seasonal change, daybreak and sunset, darkness and light, the ebb and flow of the tides, the wonders of the universe, or dances of earth, air, fire and water. Figure 3.3 shows earth shapes – the roundness of natural sculptural forms.

Figure 3.3 Earth shapes expressed in dance

The first stage in acquiring the skills to perform a dance drama is a simple narrative or story in movement, in which Reception and Key Stage 1 children mime and dance to the voice of their teacher. The more complex skills of a dance drama, which can be likened to a play without words, allow children to depict the events of a story by taking on the role of the characters in it, and by providing the mood movements for the setting of the events, as described in the previous chapter.

The characters in the dance are analysed in terms of their own movement qualities, and then these movements are practised by the children as a motif or pattern, which they subsequently arrange into sequences. Short character sketches in the first instance – for example, listening to the music and discussing the character of Grandpa in Prokofiev's *Peter and the Wolf* – will focus on movement indicators of slowness and heaviness, with spatial focus on body shape and circuitous directions, typical of Grandpa being old and unsteady on his feet. Peter, in contrast, will be quicker, firmer and more secure and confident, with a bouncy, resilient quality to his movement patterns, body shape and facial expression. Further work, linking a number of sequences together around a particular character, will yield longer sections of a dance that are easily recognised. The use of properties and items of costume add to the overall effect and pleasure of dance drama.

Masked dance is based on the notion of disguise. Children enjoy mask-making and drawing, painting or using collage materials to make images of the face. Wearing masks enables children to take on the roles of caricatures from their favourite stories and to perform scenes from stories around the world or dance dramas where the mask is part of the tradition of performance. Masks can be surrealistic, comic, tragic, or based on animal or bird designs. They can be futuristic, suggestive of space odysseys or robot dances. Shy children often gain confidence through dance when wearing a mask, and a collection of masks is an ideal classroom resource.

In addition to integrating the dance with art, music and drama, the presentation of a dance as part of a creative anthology based on a theme or topic provides curriculum cohesion. Each class will have its own repertoire of traditional dances performed on a regular basis throughout the year. Resources for English folk dances, country dances and early dance forms are readily available, while special workshops in Indian and Afro-Caribbean dance are offered by community dance artists, and regional arts centres. Professional artists working with children enhance and stimulate the cultural ethos of the primary school.

CRITICAL AWARENESS OF DANCE

Children develop critical powers in order to monitor their own performance and that of others. In this case understanding self-accomplishment through doing, and that of others through observing, is strengthened when discussed with the teacher and other children. Observing each other's work, watching a professional company which offers special programmes for young audiences, or viewing television and video programmes develops children's powers of criticism. Discourse in the classroom is constructed from a terminology of movement which teachers and children need to understand and use. Each distinctive style of dance has evolved from a specific form of movement codification, for example, the steps and gestures of classical ballet, jazz dance or Irish dance follow the rules and conventions of that particular style.

The metalanguage of dance, which describes the action and meaning of dance through verbal and written means, will be based on the terminology of dance as it relates to its elemental analysis, which are the motion factors of:

- time – indicating the rhythmic nature of movements
- energy or weight – indicating the muscular dynamics in movements
- space – indicating the pattern of movements expressed by the limbs of the body, and of the changing configurations of dancers in the performing space
- flow – indicating the fluency or constraint of movements.

Children will adapt this vocabulary to discuss:

- what their dance was about
- how they used movements to communicate what they thought and felt – levels and

directions, patterns through space, strong or light, fast or slow movements, matching movements with a partner, or formations within the group
- how they gave their dance a beginning, middle and end
- new skills and new movement sequences based on what they previously knew
- use of accompaniment – percussion, music, poem
- the patterns and figures of traditional dances, how they compare and contrast and how they can be used as a basis for their own creativity.

As children perform traditional dances they are absorbing some very interesting configurations which they can apply to their own creativity.

CONTEXTUAL AWARENESS OF DANCE

The metalanguage acquired and applied in the practical dance lessons and open class discussion in the hall is developed as discussion in the quiet area and in the written form is linked with literacy sessions. Books about dance and dancers, magazines, movement and the body, stories of the ballets, music and dance, and history and repertoire of ballet companies, will encourage reading and writing. Photographs, video and information technology, and recordings of ballet music will provide a rich cultural resource for the classroom or school library and information point. Watching a live performance of dance is a magical experience for most children and one that happens too infrequently. Major dance companies have education officers and events for children can be arranged. Touring companies from abroad also present daytime performances and workshops in schools.

THE PIVOTAL ROLE OF DANCE IN RELATION TO MUSIC, DRAMA AND ART

The temporal quality of dance relates to sound in terms of music or speech (drama, prose or poetry) in addition to movement of a rhythmical nature which could be unaccompanied. The design element based on organised shape and spatial pathways, the latter being totally illusory, lies within the visual imagination of the children, both as they perform and watch. Reference to practical examples help children to understand this imagery more clearly, for example, making patterns through the space around as if painting circles, lines or zig-zags. For the children, looking at dance they notice the tangible and clearly observable forms of the children or dancers performing, suggesting images of living statues. The rhythmic nature of movement and its dynamic content conjoins with music through such aspects as tempo, pace, metre, pulse or beat, not only in response to sounds but also as the children feel their bodies moving rhythmically. The pitch and tone of music can link up with the spatial significance of dance as expressed through the directions of movement and high, medium and low spatial levels, whether through stepping, spinning, turning, rolling, leaping in ways that defy gravity or succumb to it. The crescendo and diminuendo reflect the dynamic of perceived strength and lightness. Music and dance composition and choreography often issue from the same source or equally inspire each other and children as composers and choreographers alike determine the artistic form of the final piece.

The visual nature of dance, as expressed through shape, level and direction, appeals not only to the children's inner kinaesthetic sense as they feel the sense of movement as well as envisaging what it looks like, but there is also, from the observer's standpoint, a recognisable visual form. This is where the eyes of the children as artists are also the eyes of the children as choreographers. Watching, imagining, predicting as group formations disperse and re-form and spatial patterns expressed through gestures of limbs give rise to visual excitement and climax. In the professional theatre, the colour, the structure of the environment or performing place for the dance, whether conventional backdrop or sculptural set, is also strongly visual and imbues mood and symbolical meaning. The use of lighting schemes, costumes, masks and other artistic accoutrements when used effectively can enhance the overall choreographic presentation through harmonious integration. Children's own dance performances take place in the school hall (or community centre or church hall in the case of small village schools). Portable lighting, costumes, masks and interesting safe set constructions in the shape of lightweight screens, convoluted corrugated card or structures created from cardboard boxes are very effective and can be prepared by the children.

Dance also contains an element of drama. This can be subtly expressed through lyrical movement that embodies tension or elation of emotional expression. When children take on roles other than being themselves, then enactment and communication are used to convey both story and mood. In such instances, the dance reveals its roots with dramatic expression and akin to both music and visual art, the emotional or affective aspects of human artistic expression take on an important and crucial role. Drama, drawing upon the inspiration of comedy or tragedy, myth, belief or reality inspires dramatic interaction with the dance itself. It provides innovative responses through use of the voice – whether utterances, poetry, or dramatic dialogue that in turn may become a song lyric or libretto – and so, extending into the realms of music, artistic fusion occurs and creates a new aesthetic field. The relationship of the arts to the core area of dance is expressed in Figure 3.4.

Figure 3.4   The pivotal role of dance

ACQUIRING DANCE SKILLS

Skills training is the coalescence of science and art in the acquisition of the dance language which provides children with the means for their creativity. Children acquire coordination and control and build strength, stamina and flexibility within the safety constraints of their own physique and natural articulation of joints. Analogous with other aspects of the physical education programme, it must avoid strain, over-exertion or any unsafe practices. The body, as the major working instrument of artistic and technical expression in dance, is a vehicle of great complexity and allows children to discover new modes of movement combinations, demanding subtle changes in skill and body management. Children develop a mind/motor relationship that enables movement responses to be deduced or initiated as they use their movements to express creative ideas. Dance training prepares children to develop neuro-physiological and psychological skills in order to adjust and propel their motor energy, and mental and emotional expression into the dances they compose.

Knowing how children acquire dance skills is important. The body consists of the axial parts of head, neck and trunk, with two pairs of limbs supported by a skeletal system, the latter providing three primary functions of support, attachment of muscles and protection of organic matter (brain, spinal cord, heart and lungs). The joints or meeting points of the bones determine the type of movement possible between articulating surfaces, which vary according to the individual. Structure governs the kind and amount of movement capable in each joint and in school exaggerated and unnatural movements should be avoided.

A stimulus to movement may be the teacher's voice or the sound of the music which activates the body's response. Children's muscles, tendons and joints are excited into movement because of the reception and transmission of signals to the brain through the central nervous system. The primary motor and sensory areas of the right hemisphere of the brain control the movements of the left side of the body, and because the nerve fibres cross over to the opposite side of the brain, control of the right side of the body emanates from the left side of the brain. One side of the brain is usually more dominant than the other, and it is important to practise movements on each side of the body, allowing extra time for the weaker side.

In dance training, children develop awareness of the somesthetic sensation which includes:

- exteroceptive sensations of touch, pressure, heat, cold and pain felt from the skin
- proprioceptive sensations which indicate the tension of muscles, tendons and pressure of feet
- visceral sensation for pain and heat – this provides them with a sense of well-being and avoids exceeding pain thresholds, for example by over-exertion.

Kinaesthetic awareness is specific to skill or groups of skills as in locomotion, balance, equilibrium and body coordination. It helps the children to discriminate between the shapes of their bodies and the pathways of movement they make by way of sensations felt within the muscles, tendons and joints. Children acquire and perform their dance skills by displaying sensitivity to a number of perceptual factors including the visual, vestibular, somesthetic and kinaesthetic. Information from these sources provides knowledge of the body's orientation in space and of the spatial relationship between body parts in terms of shape and action. Perceptual skills are used extensively in the development and learning of new dance sequences while the practice and rehearsal stages draw upon motor factors. Gradually children are able to synthesise increasingly more variable postural and spatial schemata, at first as part of sequences, particularly at Key Stage 1 and then as applied to group and class dances at Key Stage 2, where the technical finesse will also be more evident. A well planned programme of study in dance will enable children to execute skilled movements which they recall, practise and perform. Practice is beneficial when it is purposeful and is effective when it is distributed throughout the week, with longer sessions as the children progress though the primary school.

Understanding the physiological development of the body through dance is important, since children's dances may contain movement sequences and sections that oscillate between a balanced stillness and fine-touch movements, or sudden, strong movements of control and vigour and slow, fine-touch movements. Some steps will involve elevation and landing, others will use the limbs to stride or leap, requiring extension or distance across the hall space. The main physiological factors to be developed as part of a skills programme in physical education will include speed, strength, agility, stamina, power, flexibility, balance, coordination and control. These important aspects will come into play throughout the entire dance lesson, and will have an impact on ways in which lessons are planned and taught.

Dance lessons commence with an introduction that focuses on the acquisition of skills. The whole class works individually performing movements that utilise:

- whole body actions and specific body parts
- immediate spatial area and use of general space
- contrasting use of motion factors (time, weight, space and flow).

In so doing, each of the above skills will incorporate major dance actions which will help the children to formulate ideas for their creative work:

- locomotion or travelling movements with emphasis on speed
- stretching, curling and twisting with emphasis on slowness
- leaping and landing with emphasis on safe take-off and landing, from one foot onto one foot
- jumping and landing safely, from two feet onto two feet
- turning
- balancing in different shapes.

Depending on the style and structure of the movement, some of which will be individual responses from the children and others prescribed by the teacher, the children exercise shoulders, elbows, wrists, fingers, spine, hips, knees, ankles, feet, toes, and neck and head. Breath control, posture and awareness of body alignment are important skills that will aid children's dance composition and performance. Introductory work focuses on:

- what the child moves – whole body actions or specific parts of the body
- where the child moves to – room space and immediate area of space
- how the child moves – the quality of movement.

Children awaken to movement by loosely shaking and slowly stretching, drawing imaginary patterns in the air, rotating their wrists or ankles and generally warming up and capturing the expectancy and excitement of dance safely. Rudolf Laban (1948) identified four main body shapes: the one-dimensional stretch resembles an arrow or steeple shape, when rib cage and arms are extended, toes are pointed and knee caps held firmly. By opening out into a wide shape, and reaching to the sides of the room the body assumes a two-dimensional shape which Laban termed a wall shape. Three-dimensional form is acquired as the body shape curls over and around into what is termed a ball shape. A gentle rotation, giving the feeling of a counter-directional pull or twisted shape will result in what Laban termed a screw shape. To add variety remember the importance of different weight-bearing parts of the body. These are the points and patches that make contact with the floor. Stillness means holding a shape like a statue. Try variations of musical statues using a percussion instrument or recorded tune.

Teaching young children to gain a sense of direction infers knowing how to explore the spatial aspects of the room confidently and effectively – whether going forwards, backwards, sideways, across, diagonally or in a circular direction – by synthesising different travelling actions. Levels mean that children experiment with rising and sinking including jumping up and falling down in a controlled way to use the floor. At any point during the lesson dance may be performed unaccompanied or to the accompaniment of music, poetry, electronic sounds or percussion, the latter possibly being played by the dancer, whether child or adult. Dances will emerge out of the discovery and study of a dance theme, and not exclusively through crafting movements to fit the musical structure. Carefully selected and appropriate pieces of music may well be used as stimuli for dance, and certainly music provides a good structure for dance improvisation.

Learning in and through dance is a bodily experience based on the absorption and expression of rhythm. A sound made from a percussion instrument can be the stimulus for dance composition. Play an instrument and ask the children to make movements that 'match the sound'. Encourage the children to listen and notice the differences of textural sounds and nuances arising from the use of different instruments. Always ensure that the children's movement response and sound reflect a close relationship. The sustained sound of the cymbal, triangle or chime bar will produce far-reaching movements, which should continue until the sound dies away. This will contrast with the sudden movements which 'match' the staccato sounds of wooden block, castanet or drum. The tambourine can accompany contrasting movements very easily by using the jingles (shaking, fluttering, flying, leaping) or the beating of the vellum (thrusting, stamping, punching, jumping). The tambour and beater is the most useful instrument for the dance lesson, and when carefully played it is able to produce sounds to accompany most dance sequences. The teacher may use a variety of instruments in any one lesson and follow themes directly related to percussion, rhythm and dance, or use them as accompaniment to movement based on an integrated topic – for example 'machines'.

A complementary use is when the children accompany their own dances. Following the National Curriculum programme for music means that musical skills of composition can be integrated with dance. Working either individually, in pairs or in groups, from an initial outburst of sounds and movements, encourage selectivity when some form of musical and dance punctuation becomes a necessity. Through phrasing and sequencing, stillness and silence, quiet and crescendo the children will soon discover their own innate and natural rhythmic tendencies, precursors for understanding received works.

action	pause	action
sound	silence	sound

As children practise their own inventions, a rhythmic study develops which to the observer will be quite different from the familiar dance timing of 4/4, 3/4 or 6/8 and will often reveal irregular timing of 5, 7 or 9 beats. Clapping, beating, stamping, clicking made with hands or feet is a successful and effective way of introducing rhythmic awareness, then moving on to holding small instruments, using the syllables, accents and beats of the child's own name. Repetitive rhythms can turn into a 'follow-the-leader' dance. Transfer the iambic, trochaic and dactylic poetry rhythms into movement sequences that will provide the basis of later work when children can base their dances on music and poetry.

Percussion instruments suitable for the dance lesson include:

drum	triangle	wood block
tambour drum	sleigh bells	rhythm sticks
side drum	Indian bells	Chinese temple block
tambourine	jingle sticks	maracas
cymbals	claves	chime bars

- Use a good quality tambour as your main accompaniment.
- Use a selection of six to ten percussion instruments for group work.
- Select instruments that the children can hold and play as they dance.
- Select fairly short pieces of music with distinctive sounds reflective of the qualities of movement in the dance.
- Acquire a repertoire of music involving solo instruments that offer contrasting textures of sounds and rhythms: strings – violin, piano, harpsichord; woodwind – clarinet, oboe, bassoon; brass – trumpets, trombone, horn.
- Use electronic sounds.
- Use instrumental music from different cultures – native American, native Australian, Chinese, Japanese, Afro-Caribbean and Indian music.
- Use selections of pop music and popular pieces e.g. sound from *The Snowman*.
- Use tapes especially recorded for dance with children in a creative way.
- Use live music – pianist, school orchestra, guest musicians – when possible.

Sound accompaniment can be varied and stimulating, and needs to be introduced with sensitivity. Sounds can match movements and movements can respond to sounds. Use a variety of sounds, whether recorded or percussion, including electronic and sounds from diverse cultural sources. Self-accompaniment means that children play percussion instruments and dance either on their own or with a partner. When using percussion start with rhythmical sound using the tambour which is the first and foremost instrument. Then progressively work from this to include soft bells, tambourine, wooden blocks, triangle and chime bars.

Free response to music, whether at the start or end of a lesson, allows the children to become absorbed in their own creativity and expression by building on their understanding and performance skills, week by week, and encourages an appreciation of music. Keep choices simple and rhythmical. Poetry and prose can be used effectively in dance sessions, so use rhymes, poetry, jingles, and work from sounds and alliteration. In all dance teaching the use of the imagination is paramount. Make good use of metaphor and simile, and draw in imagery that links to stories, poems, visits and the environment, so that dance is firmly rooted in the curriculum as a whole and endorses other modes of learning.

CHOREOGRAPHY AND DANCE

Children's dance skills facilitate their creativity, which is about inventing or composing dances. The prime motivational factor for dance composition is movement associated with ideas, so when children invent dances they are applying kineasthetic intelligence since their dances are based on neuromuscular responses in which they have successfully unified idea and the structural expression. Choreography – derived from the Greek word *choreia* (a choral dance) and *graphia* (writing) – is a specific term which defines the composition of dances. A literal interpretation implies the writing of dances. Dance composition is a synonymous term which can also refer to the preparatory experiences when children experiment and build up their short sequences, and phrases from which they gain their experiences for creating a complete dance. This takes place with the help of the teacher and other children in the class and grows out of the preliminary stages of individual work.

The child's creative role as choreographer is expressed through the following channels:

- the body as the instrument of dance expression
- individual, partner work or group dances
- spatial element indicating group shape, movement motif and spatial design, floor pathways of individuals and groups (directions)
- dynamic element indicating the colouring and shading of spatial forms
- rhythmic element indicating the continuation, halting and changing flow of movement.

A number of factors help in understanding the development of choreographic skills, the fundamental one being how the teacher can stimulate or motivate children for movement. Figure 3.5 shows the cooperation through partner work at Key Stage 1, by creating bridges and moving over, under and around each other. Being excited about the dance's subject and having an awareness of the appropriateness of the idea for expression through movement is important, since each art form has it limitations. In the preparatory stages of the lesson children will experiment with ideas using intuitive responses, developing awareness and understanding of their bodies as the means of expressing ideas. The neuromuscular responses are to some degree guided by kinetic intuition linked with idea of what the dance is about. The coalescence of body and mind are important factors when children are thinking in terms of movement through action as they create their dances, since the body and its movement is implacably implanted within the artifact.

Figure 3.5   A study of partner work in dance

In the first instance, this is expressed through the establishment of the basic movement motif or design as it is developed into sequential form and longer movement phrases and passages of a dance. In group work it includes the coordination and interrelationships between all the children in the group that allow them to think collectively and work harmoniously together. Teaching strategies can facilitate this by setting individual leadership tasks within the group for all its members.

The structural organisation and adaptation of movements introduced and experienced at the start of the dance lesson provides opportunity for children to invent new combinations of movements they already know. Children can also experiment with new movement motifs and new arrangements of them. A third possibility is linking the new with the known, which underlies most artistic experiences.

Creative work in dance is determined by a number of organising factors including group shapes. Some choreographic group shapes are derived from historical sources including children's singing games and folk dance forms which provide excellent reference points for choreographers. Dance groups are constantly unfolding and changing and include the circle, the row (straight line), rank and file, and symmetrical or asymmetrical group shapes that allow children to be clustered together or widely spaced. Sometimes, when making a tableau shape come alive, as in *tableau vivant*, the shape is determined by an object – a windmill, a boat, the selfish giant's garden, giant whale – and the structural form is based on representational ideas and the way children envisage and organise group shapes.

Group shapes will change constantly – as one shape disintegrates another re-forms. Figure 3.6 depicts an elongated, monster shape on a theme of metamorphosis. A group following a leader to a different location in the room, then adapting to a new shape, works successfully, as do groupings when the children work in unison together, or in contrast with each other. Ideas for dispersing groups and conglomerating groups can be used to express a scientific concept. The group shape is determined by the content of the dance, as for example dancing robots in rank and file, or a rectangular shape of a machine.

Figure 3.6 Group shape based on an imaginary monster

A dance about electricity has the following choreographic structure:

- making the electricity depicted as a group shape representing a power station as a tall chimney, giant cooling towers or generating plant
- transmitting the electricity through pylons – follow-the-leader with rhythmical stepping, jumping and springing, sharp and jagged movements of arms, each child taking turns to lead
- using the electricity – dancing the motions of a domestic appliance – actions and group shape of washing machine, toaster, dishwasher, etc.

Choreographic group shapes commence as soon as children are formed into a circle shape and develop at Reception and Key Stage 1 as whole-class experiences when children respond to the teacher. Independent group work, when children learn to work with each other, is introduced and developed at Key Stage 2.

Dance is a temporal art form, so it follows that the changing visual configurations are also linked with the rhythmical structure of the dance. Children develop ideas and organise their own rhythmical structure of sequences and phrases of dance. Sound accompaniment is also a way of providing organisational structure to dance composition whether it is the spoken word, as in poetry, or music. Some musical forms can be interpreted in dance. Unison implies all members of the group or class dancing in time to the music. Canon will differentiate, so that some patterns and levels of movement will match or correspond to pitch and rhythm of music. A rondo implies groups, or individuals within the group beginning and ending sequentially. Children will develop their own contemporary style of movement as individuals, inventing dances that are original and vibrant – some processes will be experimental. When they perform dances from existing cultures, they will reflect the style of the dance, for example traditional folk dances of Great Britain.

In addition to creative dance leading to a choreographic performance and critical understanding, children require to experience its cultural and historical aspects in a practical way. Britain's vast and beautiful heritage provides a rich and stimulating resource. Not only are there many places to visit, but music, literature, drama, and art works in museums, galleries and stately homes give opportunity for the interpretative and creative qualities of dance.

RECONSTRUCTION OF DANCES

The country dance was the ordinary, everyday dance of country-folk, performed on festal days and whenever opportunity arose. Performed in couples (partners of opposite sexes), the steps and figures are simple and easily learned. The English Folk Dance and Song Society currently produce teaching packs with music and descriptions of dances. Folk dances have set figures of varying complexity, and simple rhythmical steps which children over generations have successfully mastered. A useful start to the lesson is to get the children to skip, gallop or polka step to a particular piece of music, sometimes in a circle, dancing round the room anticlockwise following the line of dance, sometimes following a leader round the room, making a serpentine pattern en route and then holding a partner by the hand and dancing round the room together. The boy will take his partner with his right hand. Steps are light and resilient to the floor, backs are held straight, and the children acquire a sense of happy, control and respect for each other. The figures which are appropriate for children at Key Stage 2 include longways sets, square sets, quadrille, and circle dances. The following ten dances are appropriate for Key Stage 2 classes.[2]

Brighton Camp
Music: 'Brighton Camp'
Formation: Longways set for four to eight couples

Cumberland Long Eight
Music: Reel or jig tune
Formation: Longways set for four couples, boy facing girl

Circassian Circle (Part 2)
Music: 'Good Humour'
Formation: A ring of any size, girl on boy's right

Cumberland Square Eight
Music: 'My Love's She But a Lassie Yet', or any reel or jig tune
Formation: Quadrille (top and side couples dance consecutively)

Blaydon Races Mixer
Music: 'Blaydon Races'
Formation: Any number of couples in circle

Cross Hands or Bonnets so Blue
Music: 'Bonnets so Blue'
Formation: Longways duple minor progressive dance

Butterfly
Music: 'The Butterfly'
Formation: Longways duple minor progressive dance

Double Schottishe – Devonshire
'One, two, three, four, five, six, seven,
All good children go to heaven,
Penny on the water, tuppence on the sea,
Three pence on the roundabouts, and
    round go we,
Penny on the water, tuppence on the sea,
Three pence on the roundabouts, and
    round go we.'
Formation: Partner dance, ballroom hold.
Chassé four times anticlockwise
Chassé four times clockwise
Chassé twice anticlockwise
Chassé twice clockwise
Waltz turning (clockwise rotation)
Repeat two chassés anticlockwise
Chassé twice clockwise, waltz turning
(The children should sing as they dance)

The Cumberland Reel
Music: 'Cumberland Reel' or any other reel, jig or hornpipe
Formation: Long set for four or more couples – boy facing partner

The Tempest (Wiltshire)
Music: 'The Tempest'
Formation: Progressive double quadrille
Four couples = a set
Two couples facing two couples

The standard of performance of dances will vary, from the best possible at the end of a lesson, to a higher standard if performed as the culmination of two or three lessons a specially rehearsed dance for presentation to a wider audience than peers. Keeping in time to the music, remembering the dances, making eye contact with partners, and holding hands respectfully are social as well as artistic skills that children acquire through this

2. The collecting, recording and dissemination of English folk dances into schools was instigated by Cecil J. Sharp (1859–1924).

dance style. They obtain harmony, become aware of each other, and derive joy and satisfaction with each dancing partner, especially during dances that involve new partners. Traditional dances can be performed on social occasions in the school, perhaps at summer fêtes or times when parents and friends are able to join in celebrations.

TRADITIONAL DANCES AND CREATIVITY

Support and resources for teachers from local arts organisations will enable professional dancers and teachers to bring expertise to schools. There are strong links between the experience of performing existing dances and the way in which children can utilise these experiences when they invent their own dances. By recognising the form of dances, their musical structure, and the way in which they dance in time to the music, children are able to grasp the rudiments of choreography. The way in which children work together, helping each other and changing partners, encourages interaction and the exchange of ideas within creative contexts. Aesthetic, social and personal education are developed through the courtesy and mutual respect that social dances require. Traditional dances can be adapted and interpreted for use in drama lessons, or linked with visits to stately homes or museums.

EMBODIMENT AS A MAJOR MODE OF LEARNING

Embodiment is when ideas or concepts are given a discernible form. Children use dance movements as a form of communication, expressing what they understand through the content of their dances. In so doing, they demonstrate how their ideas and images have been absorbed within themselves as a valid and meaningful two-way process, comparable with the conceptual understanding of other types of arts languages. In the initial stages they will take their lead from the teacher who will encourage the use of shape, movement patterns, relationships and dynamics to portray ideas and concepts. The more adept children are in their skills of dance, the more eloquent they become in the way in which they conceptualise through dance movements. Dancing out ideas and concepts, given the means of communication, is a logical and valid mode of learning which is accessible to children. It is not 'pretending' to be, but rather 'expressing the idea'. Children demonstrate how they concretise ideas through dance when they portray the characters in a story, or when they invent dances that involve the understanding of a scientific, historical, geographical or technological concept. Chapter 6 ('The Interrelated Curriculum Mode') provides a number of exemplars using this principle.

One exemplar dance project undertaken with children at Reception to Key Stages 1 and 2 is based on Diwali (the Hindu festival of lights) and demonstrates how the tradition of dance and drama can be applied creatively as part of an integrated arts mode. Planning for dance requires a clear vision of what is to take place, ensuring the content is appropriate for the age and experience of the children. Well balanced and developmental material, working from the known experience and introducing new ideas will also incorporate skills and improved responses and attainment each week as children gain more confidence in working creatively together.

The story popularly associated with the festival of Diwali is that of Prince Rama and his wife Princess Sita, who, after a series of adventures, confrontations with evil, and imposed exile, return to their kingdom, welcomed by the glow of lamps lit by their subjects. Diwali means 'cluster of lights' and is the New Year celebration associated with the Hindu and Sikh religions. Celebrated during the four days at the end of October and the beginning of November, it marks the end of harvest and the start of the new year. New Year's Day is celebrated by visiting friends and relatives, exchanging gifts, and decorating homes with colourful rangoli patterns.

The story is available in special children's editions, many with colourful illustrations, and can be read or told to the children. The material and approaches of this exemplar also provide a workable framework for the treatment of most stories that lead to either a dance-drama, a mime play, or a multi-media event in which children use movement, voice, musical instruments and wear masks and simple costumes. The story can be adapted for use with either Key Stage 1 or 2 classes. In the former there would be a requirement for more teacher input and progress would be at a slower rate, while in the latter a greater degree of child autonomy is both possible and desirable, with greater sophisticated skills and artistry through independent group work. Rehearsal and practice are necessary for performance purposes. Critical appraisal and discussion are important aspects, both from the stance of participant and observer. The following scenario, with suggested teaching approaches, can be adapted for different ages of children, with selected scenes or presentation of the whole story.

The Ramayana

The characters in the story are Prince Rama, Princess Sita, Ravana the demon king, Hanuman the leader of the monkey army, the golden deer and animals of the forest.

- Make a movement analysis of each character – shape, pattern, dynamic.
- Teach specific skills – body part, whole body.
- Let children create sequences of movements portraying the characters.

Prince Rama is brave and good. He will ride his horse over mountains and valleys and into the forest where he will fight off evil monsters. The emphasis is on strong, powerful movements with good body carriage and stepping and galloping movements as he rides his horse through the mountains. Agile movements, such as leaping, jumping, and thrusting, should be used when he fights off the demons of the forest but slow, controlled movements when he meets Princess Sita. Use the tambour for accompaniment.

Princess Sita is beautiful, kind and affectionate. Create a partner dance for Princess Sita and Prince Rama using meeting and parting as the theme based on mirror images (matching movements facing) and shadow images (based on follow-the-leader when each character will take turns to move first and follow). Partners should hold hands, turn and play hide-and-seek in the forest to represent travelling and arriving on the different pathways through the forest. There should be speed variations and contrasting of dynamics. Develop patterns and style based on hands and feet leading and matching, travelling and arriving into statuesque shapes using tambour and chime bars for accompaniment.

Ravana is the ten-headed demon king – wicked, strong and cunning, full of rage and anger. Use strong movements that twist and turn, sometimes slow and sinister, sometimes angry and sudden. Practise a sequence which includes turning, rolling, leaping and contrast this with slow pressing movements as Ravana struggles to break through the magic circle which wards off evil. After working individually, portray Ravana as a small group. Use a drum and cymbal, or rasp sound.

The golden deer is magical and looks enchanting but tricks Princess Sita. Start with the quick, light and agile movements. Sudden and lively footwork, springing, resilient movements to the sound of bells. Practise changing from the golden deer into the demon monster.

Hanuman is helpful, fearless, the leader of a resourceful army. Devise a pounding, rhythmical sequence of sideways travelling, leaping and pouncing, repeated in both left and right directions. Work individually and then as a small group representing the monkey army. Hanuman and the monkey army help to build a palace in the middle of the forest, and then a bridge or causeway linking the main land of India to Lanka.

Use patterns, shapes and *tableau vivant* to depict the locations of the dance drama:

- Landscape of the mountains and forests of India – using fingertips delineate the silhouettes of mountains, valleys and steep slopes. Depict the rock and valley shapes using individuals and pairs.
- The palace in the forest clearing – in circular formation use statuesque shapes representative of windows, colonnades, domes, statues, doors, inner circle higher and enclosure.
- The sea around Lanka and the raging storm – delineate the calm sea (horizontal), wavy sea and storm, using a sequence of high, medium, and low levels leading to leaping and turning.
- The great bridge or causeway linking India with Lanka – use either two lines of children facing each other, moving backwards and lifting into a wave like shape and stillness creating the causeway, or use two lines of children facing each other with hands linked, making a bridge.
- Ravana's palace garden where Princess Sita is imprisoned – use a variation of a circle formation as a group, encircling Sita.

The Meeting of Prince Rama and Princess Sita

Prince Rama and his courtiers journey through the mountains and into the forest which they clear of the demons. They come across a clearing and Prince Rama meets Princess Sita. Hanuman, king of the monkey army along with elephants, tigers, birds, and snakes help to build the palace. Mime collecting the stone and timber and constructing the palace. Prince Rama uses his bow and arrow to make a magic circle around the palace to keep evil at bay. He waves goodbye to Princess Sita and disappears into the forest.

Ravana the Demon King

Ravana desires to have Princess Sita as his queen but he cannot pass through the magic circle. Thwarted at not being able to get into the palace he skulks back into the forest and then disguises himself as a golden deer. The deer dances and lures Princess Sita beyond the protection of the magic circle. He captures her and changes back into his monstrous form.

The Rescue

Prince Rama returns and is frantic when he cannot find Princess Sita. He and his brother Lakshman search the whole of India for her. Having told them that Sita is imprisoned in Lanka, Hanuman flies through the air taking Rama's ring to Sita, promising her she will be rescued. On his return, Hanuman and the monkey army build a bridge across the ocean. (In some versions of the story the god of the ocean creates a great storm and makes the waves part revealing a causeway on the ocean bed.) The army, led by Prince Rama, Lakshman and Hanuman cross the bridge into Lanka. They overcome the demons and Prince Rama, carrying his magic bow and arrow, confronts Ravana and a battle between them takes place (do not allow physical contact). Each time Prince Rama lashes out with his sword and swipes off a head, two more sprout! Eventually, as the will of the gods, he fires an arrow into Ravana who falls dead to the ground. He frees Princess Sita from her prison.

The Festival of Light

Amid great rejoicing a procession, headed by Prince Rama, Princess Sita, Lakshman and all the animals and villagers, winds its way across the forests and plains and mountains, bright lanterns revealing the conquest of good over evil. End with the re-forming of the palace.

THE RECORDING AND REPORTING OF DANCE EXPERIENCES WITH CHILDREN

The recording and reporting of dance lessons relates very closely to the critical understanding of the art form, both from the perspective of the child and the teacher. All the practical experiences of dance offered to children will lead to a greater understanding of dance, as art form and as social pastime since the two activities of doing and viewing dances are closely interrelated. This is especially true when the criteria for viewing corresponds with the criteria for doing, as set out below:

- what my dance will be about – indicates the appropriate choice of ideas
- how my ideas will be presented – making an overview of the performance
- how I express myself – working out the precise nature of the movements i.e. the rhythm, the dynamics, the pattern, the fluency
- the form the dance takes – working out the precise use of group formations and style that helps to convey the idea
- how skilful my dance is – indicating how the content challenges current levels
- the symbolical meaning of my dance
- what aesthetic qualities are in my dance.

When children invent their dances with a clear understanding of what is expected of them they are able to build upon these experiences in order to discuss and write about dance critically and contextually. Improvement takes place when children are encouraged to think through their dances, either as a silent inactive preparation in the hall, or as a contemplative written activity in class.

When children view dance it will be in terms of:

- what the dance was about – indicating the effectiveness of communicating ideas
- how the ideas were presented
- making an overview of the performance
- how the ideas were expressed – identifying the precise nature of the observed movements i.e. the rhythm, the dynamics, the pattern, the fluency
- forms that were used – noting the precise use of group formations and style used to convey the ideas in the dance
- how skilfully the dance was performed – noting body management and execution of specific movements
- how the aesthetic qualities were conveyed in the dance – noting the overall response to the performance.

As with drama, children's progress in dance can be recorded at intervals as required by the school. It will be based on observational notes relating to each individual project, and along with drama and music will provide an aesthetic and artistic profile in performance arts for individual children.

CHAPTER 4

The Music Mode

Music has the ability to enhance and intensify the other art forms yet contains an intensive degree of intellectual and emotional content within its own right. The music context develops the manipulation of sound sources in ways which convey meaning and communicate ideas and understanding of the aural world, impressing upon the listener changes in moods, imagination and emotional states. The earth – wind, forest, plains and mountains of the world – has provided inspiration for composers and every conceivable location has been, or can be, the auditorium for music. Villages, streets, churches, courts, concert hall, markets, arenas and sports stadia have been and still are venues for the celebration of music. The onset of the gramophone, radio, and electronic recording of music has revolutionised its accessibility and children today enter into and grow up in an intensive world of sound and music.

Music in the primary school curriculum seeks to develop an understanding of the art form along two strands, of which the first involves situations that develop a strong understanding of the basic elements of music. The second strand encompasses the appreciation, historical and cultural context along with critical listening skills and the development of all other attendant aspects of music. It is important to remember that it is the interrelationship between a number of salient musical factors that results in music and it is impossible to deal with any single ingredient individually.

Children are required to develop musical concepts. This can be considered as similar to the way early learning develops number concepts by handling the raw elements of numeracy in many varied, practical and structured ways. This diverse approach is effective and inclusive for the maximum number of children. Teachers encourage children to play with the notion of counting and are fully aware of the point when these structured early activities have brought about the conceptualisation of addition or subtraction. Effective teachers engineer the learning environment to maximise these learning strategies. It is acknowledged that as part of the process of presentation music is both played and played with, in order to develop the skill and understanding levels which manifest as rehearsal and performance.

In addition to the development of musical concepts, children are also learning to be conversant in a creative language within the context of a system used for the conveyance of information. Music is a universal language and the information it conveys is understood by people around the world. The building blocks of this language are common to a global audience. Music has the ability to enhance experience or strengthen the meaning of other activities. All societies and cultures make extensive use of music in this accompanying role, with examples ranging from festivals, celebrations and rituals through to film sound tracks, partying and shopping.

Entwined within the universal language aspect of music is the specific technical language of the art form. Running throughout the developmental process of the music curriculum is a structure which calls for greater levels of sophistication from the children in terms of how they acquire and understand this specific language. There is a commonality between all art forms, which will assist in developing degrees of descriptive comment related to integrated arts projects. It is important to focus on the creative and aesthetic development of children as a partnership with the safer areas of rudiments and technique.

Considerable energy is devoted toward contextualising all forms of education to make learning fun, interesting and enjoyable. Musical activities, naturally, have these rejuvenating qualities built into them. Some children will find an opportunity to excel in musical communication while others will be highly motivated by musical activities. It is important to acknowledge that such a powerful educational tool is seen within the context of crossing the boundaries of all curriculum areas as well as holding its own discrete right. Within a highly structured National Curriculum it is vital to realise that schemes, plans and lessons are required which deliver a broader and balanced style of education. This is linked to the understanding of how vital such work can be in enriching children's lives and that of their school and community.

THE TEACHING AND LEARNING FRAMEWORK FOR MUSIC

The National Curriculum for Music provides a good structure for children's work and is designed to be very practical and accessible for children and teachers alike. The structure remains unified through all key stages and, since it revision in 2000, has a commonality with other subjects. It calls for children to sing, play instruments, rehearse and perform, respond, create and explore, actively listen and apply knowledge with understanding. The intention is to also build children's confidence in these areas as they progress.

Teaching music as part of an integrated arts model is based on its artistic, aesthetic, critical and cultural aspects with the programme of study for music running parallel with those for dance, drama and visual art. Similarly, as means of endorsing the unity of learning in the arts, the areas of study will include:

- participation in music – children's practical knowledge of music through performance
- repertoire of music – children's accumulative knowledge shown in the music they can perform
- critical skills of music – children's knowledge of the qualities and special nature of music experienced through music-making and listening to music, and expressed through discussion and writing
- context of music – children's knowledge of the historical, social and cultural worlds that have inspired or informed their understanding of music.

Figure 4.1 is a diagrammatic presentation of this working theory and includes the key issues for each area of knowledge.

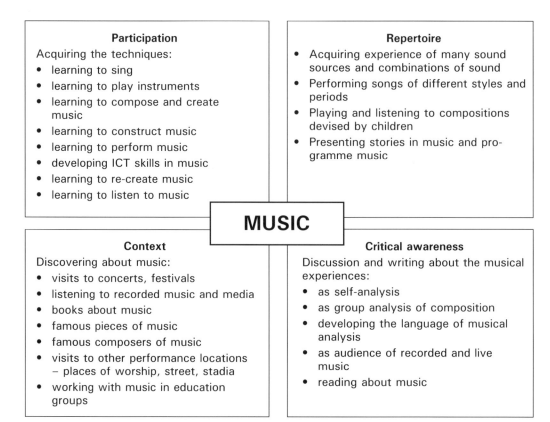

Participation

Acquiring the techniques:

- learning to sing
- learning to play instruments
- learning to compose and create music
- learning to construct music
- learning to perform music
- developing ICT skills in music
- learning to re-create music
- learning to listen to music

Repertoire

- Acquiring experience of many sound sources and combinations of sound
- Performing songs of different styles and periods
- Playing and listening to compositions devised by children
- Presenting stories in music and programme music

MUSIC

Context

Discovering about music:

- visits to concerts, festivals
- listening to recorded music and media
- books about music
- famous pieces of music
- famous composers of music
- visits to other performance locations – places of worship, street, stadia
- working with music in education groups

Critical awareness

Discussion and writing about the musical experiences:

- as self-analysis
- as group analysis of composition
- developing the language of musical analysis
- as audience of recorded and live music
- reading about music

Figure 4.1   A framework for the teaching and learning of music

Music education is strongly practical and from the Reception class onwards children are taught to acquire the necessary skills for their creative and interpretive expression. This entails learning to sing, learning to play appropriate instruments and using them to create musical compositions. Listening is fundamental, both in terms of the sounds individuals produce and also the collective responses of groups and the class as a whole. As children work their way through each year group they will build up a personal repertoire of music, often shared with their peers. In addition to their own compositions, the repertoire will include items from the established musical repertoire, as appropriate to age and development.

Discovering about the many contexts in which musical activities can be found relies upon personal experiences of live music as well as accessing selections from electronic music libraries. Listening to and appreciating music is experienced in many ways, not necessarily as part of a music lesson but also in school assembly or perhaps through movement interpretation as part of the dance lesson. Critical awareness, often implicit within the creative aspects of music-making, in terms of how children understand the nature of their practical experiences is expressed through discussion and writing, and through gathering information about music.

PARTICIPATION IN MUSIC

Musical elements provide the substance of most activities and are defined within each key stage in appropriate language for the different age groups. The elements are: pitch, duration (including rhythm), dynamics, tempo, timbre, texture and structure and form. Children are required to gain an understanding of these elements alongside the ability to use them in creating moods and effects. Imaginative association, narrative and relationships with other concepts are important learning techniques in this context. Targets for the end of each key stage provide guidelines for assessment and progression with children. The current version of the Music National Curriculum simplifies assessment and enables greater flexibility in the selection of activities thus assisting the teacher to integrate musical activities and to combine the programmes of study when and where possible. Teaching programmes will inevitably strike a balance of content phased over the two- or four-year period related to each key stage respectively.

The seven musical elements, individually, hold different levels of complexity. Pitch and rhythm are the most difficult areas in which to gain competence and establish themselves as the two elements demanding most time and energy. The knowledge base is less in the other areas, however, it is important to realise that degrees of parity exist in the interplay between several musical elements as a piece of music is performed. An order for handling the elements of music would commence with timbre and progress through to specific pitch.

Timbre

Timbre relates to the different types of sound and how differing sounds can be produced. Discovery and exploration will present the children with opportunities to experiment with a musical sound source. The first part of this experimentation involves the mechanics related to producing the sound and the variations available from it. For example, a large drum can be played at any point between the edge or in the centre of the skin – the tension of the skin and the composition of the beater and the style of the stroke all affect the tonal quality. The rim and shell of the drum will also produce interesting sounds, which all together provide a kaleidoscope of tonal qualities for compositional use.

Combining the different tonal qualities of any instrument or group of instruments into a piece creates a structure for compositional work and provides the framework for the exploration of this quality. The second stage of the exploration involves the development of ideas related to imaginative thought association – 'When the drum plays like this it could be a …'. This section encourages children to use descriptive language to describe sound and indicate any thoughts about moods and emotions related to the sound. This permits discursive, pictorial, dramatic, written or kinaesthetic responses.

At Key Stage 2 the children could conduct similar work using a virtual analogue synthesiser program on the computer. VAZ+ (free demo version available to download from the Internet) presents a screen filled with virtual sliders and switches that control different components of the overall sound. The children can choose a single note and then proceed to move the sliders, gradually, while hearing the sound change. The sliders and switches are specifically labelled and the topic presents a suitable launching pad into science, ICT (information and communications technology) and music links. At an exploratory level the children can access electronic workshop sounds. In both examples the children will produce music which can be performed as stand-alone pieces or as an accompaniment to other activities. Electronic composition of this nature provides exciting accompaniment for the reciting of a poem, while the drum study presents the opportunity to express ideas in movement.

Texture

In the context of music, texture relates to how many musical events are happening at the same time. A solo soprano voice would provide a light texture, but as a four-part choir joins the soloist the texture becomes richer as the different vocal parts fill in the spectrum of pitch ranges. A string section then joins the singers and adds a thicker texture to the music, and so on. The descriptive language is borrowed from other contexts which is true for any attempt to convey information about the arts. It is important for the children to engage in this dialogue to establish and develop an understanding of the language required within this context. Knowledge of the language will also assist in developing the practical aspects of music used in compositional work. The feelings of sadness in a piece of music could be reflected by the use of a plaintive light texture incorporating a sombre melodic line in a minor key. The children learn how to exercise discernment related to the instruments used by how they are combined, how others have utilised them and how these things can be emulated in their own work.

Form

Music is highly structured and usually conforms to a plan. At a simple level this can be a beginning, middle and end. Songs can be structured as verses and choruses or just verses. The structure becomes a form of logic which helps with the overall sense of a piece of music. Many structures provide a way of extending musical ideas and linking together a number of threads, themes or ideas. Rondo form has a construction where a musical theme reoccurs and is interspaced with different themes. A musical journey could be represented by a vehicle travelling through a town. The travellers stop at the market square, they then travel on to a place of worship, ride to the canal and finish their journey with a visit at the park before returning home. The rondo shape is represented by:

journey music
market music
journey music
place of worship music
journey music
canal music
journey music
park music
journey music

The journey music provides a logical structure which presents familiarity and security for performer and listener alike. The structure also serves to extend the composition by recycling previous ideas. Pop songs frequently use four bars which are repeated many times over as a harmonic structure. A samba rhythm style on a keyboard playing two bars based on the chord of C followed by two bars on the chord of F would provide the harmonic structure. A steady two-bar melody, giving the feel of music asking a question, followed by two more bars, giving the feeling of an answer, provides the verse. Increase the word rate and create a four-bar melody based on the same repeating chords to construct a chorus. A spoken four-bar rap provides an interlude. The overall song structure then becomes:

chorus
verse
chorus
interlude
verse
chorus and interlude [together]
chorus

Style and chordal accompaniments for this level of work are also available within keyboards and as computer software packages. Using these programs allows the computer to display musical events as coloured blocks, which can then be copied and pasted. The resultant edition is a colourful visual and aural representation of the song structure. Pleasing results can be produced quickly because of the way technology can recycle musical ideas. These techniques are very common in pop and film music.

Duration

A substantial amount of work related to how music deals with time is represented under this heading of duration. Synchronisation is required between a number of performers to establish good starts and endings and also to signal events happening along the way. Synchronisation is also fundamental in appreciating and responding to a regular pulse. Once the players are able to start and stop the music together, a common pulse has to be established. Musical skills require children to accomplish several tasks at the same time, which is achieved by scanning each activity in turn and making adjustments as necessary.

Some children initially wrestle to appreciate a regular pulse because they are still developing the ability to understand things of an abstract nature. Listening is at the heart of feeling the pulse and it is usually 'caught' as opposed to taught. Plenty of exposure will allow the children to focus on a steady pulse and thereby 'catch it'. Other children can respond to a steady pulse almost without thinking, establishing a foundation to hold the music together which acts as a model and form of security enabling others to join in. Group music-making is effectively enhanced by solid pulse work and is a precursor to more complex rhythm work. The speed of the pulse sets the pace of the music. Beats within the steady pulse receive different levels of accentuation and, linked with pace, they have a strong bearing on the mood of the piece.

Rhythm

Longer, more complex and faster patterns provide a continuum of rhythmic complexities reaching almost into infinity. Rhythmic patterns provide excitement and interest in relation to the steady pulse. The first beat of a bar is always a strong beat. The following rhythm has an African feel which is achieved by adding an additional strong beat at the end of the bar [stand – play]. It lends itself to three drums and should be repeated over and over. Figure 4.2 shows how it is expressed in words and the conventional music notation is shown in Figure 4.3. The music is divided into measures of four beats. Measures with three beats tend to evoke side-to-side movement, as shown in Figure 4.4. With a very slow pulse a lullaby effect is achieved (Figure 4.5). Moving the pulse a little faster, as shown in Figure 4.6, indicates the movement of a boat. This sequence exemplifies that in order to capture changes in musical feel there is a corresponding change in pace.

	play	me	now.	Oh	won't	you	stand	and	play	me	now.	Oh	won't	you	stand	and	
stand	play						stand		play						stand		play
	one		two		three		four		one		two		three		four		

Figure 4.2   Rhythmic patterns expressed in words

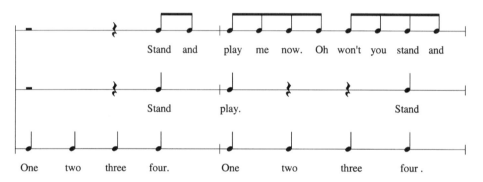

Figure 4.3   Rhythmic patterns expressed in music notation

Figure 4.4   Measure with three beats

Go to sleep lit - tle babe.

Figure 4.5 A slow pulse creates a lullaby effect

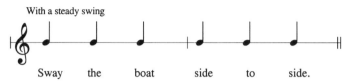

Sway the boat side to side.

Figure 4.6 A faster pulse indicates the movement of a boat

The children develop a rhythmic sense as they experience regular pulses of differing speeds by the inclusion of subdivisions of measures containing accented notes and all underlying rhythmic patterns. The permutations change in relationship to the style of the music and the level of vigour required.

Pitch

Musical instruments produce vibrations in the air and the frequency of these vibrations varies in relation to pitch. The faster the vibration the higher the note and conversely, the slower the vibration the lower the pitch. Instruments capable of producing low sounds are large and few of them are available to primary-aged children because of the incompatibility between small children and large instruments.

Pitch also relates to hearing a note and being able to reproduce it with some accuracy using the voice. Aural skills are developed by practice, careful listening and encouragement to internalise sound. Pitch is developed by increasing the repertoire of songs and also by encouraging the children to listen and copy as they develop physical control over their voices alongside the aural skills. Developing a sense of pitch can take time for some children, while others appear to have it instinctively. It is important to remember that internalising sound is a learned skill – practice increases the range of notes all children are able to pitch. Human voices lean towards one of four ranges in adult life: soprano, alto, tenor and bass. Physically, primary-aged children's voices are capable of reproducing frequencies, somewhere between alto and soprano ranges, once they have developed the ability to place their voice.

Children will develop the ability to distinguish between high notes and low notes starting from a situation where the notes are far apart and moving to a situation where they become adjacent notes. This is established by monitoring the distinction between separate single sounds and progresses on to include discrimination between several events happening at the same time. Careful listening and experience are required to improve the ability to discriminate between sounds of differing pitch. The note g played on a recorder and then a xylophone may be perceived as different to the listener although they are exactly the same frequency. The difference is related to the tonal quality of the sound, not the pitch. All human senses recognise and respond to a change of stimulus, consequently the senses tend to block out or not even notice constant stimuli.

Musical composition often relates high and low. It would be most peculiar to watch someone ascending a flight of stairs accompanied by a melody that gradually descended in pitch. The expectation of pitch ascending, as a visual image moves higher, is almost a conditioned response. This response is not necessarily acknowledged when it comes to the conventions of producing sounds on an instrument. Keyboards have keys of two different lengths and equate low-pitched notes to the left and progressing to the high on the right. Xylophones have the same convention with the added indicator of endorsing that long equals low, and short equals high. A recorder or clarinet fits a vertical model of pitch relationship and would further endorse the ascending of a flight of stairs scenario. Employing these relationships within compositional work enhances the understanding of pitch.

High and low are very subjective terms that are quickly adjusted to circumstances. The lowest note on a small school glockenspiel could be considered as a high note in relationship to the lowest note on a bass xylophone. Delivering the music curriculum will require the children to develop an understanding of pitch across the entire compass of human hearing, and the application of relationships will facilitate many creative opportunities when combining work with the other arts, especially with dance.

Music has a number of theoretical techniques related to pitch which will form a basis for all the children's 'tuned' musical experiences. The body of knowledge includes: pentatonic scales, major scales, minor scales, whole-tone scales and restricted scales. These scales provide characteristic 'flavours' in the music and become the tools to assist the children with their practical music-making. An example of this would be to create music for a medieval dance, first of all by playing a drone on a keyboard (notes **a** and **e**) with a cello voice to a repeated rhythmic pattern of 'court danc-ers'. Add a tambour playing the same rhythm and complete the piece with a recorder making up a melody using part of a scale **g**, **a**, **b**, **c** and only settling for any length of time on note **a** or **c**. Figure 4.7 shows the musical notation. Change the drone notes to **f** and **c**, leave the rhythm the same and change the melody notes to become **f**, **f#**, **b flat** and **b**, settling for any length of time only on note **f**. Now the music possesses an Eastern flavour. The musical notation is presented in Figure 4.8.

All theoretical knowledge is related to assisting the children to produce music of their own in an educated way. It forms bridges of access and is intended to facilitate rapid entry to the complicated field of concordant musical harmony while allowing some creative freedom. Predetermining a pentatonic scale as the building block for a composition allows

Figure 4.7 Recorder melodic notes and drone notes **a** and **e** using cello voice on keyboard

Figure 4.8   Melody notes and drone notes **f** and **c**

the children to invent a number of tunes that sound good together. The tunes can also be built up in layers to increase the texture of a composition. This is achieved by the removal of all the notes **b** and **e** which leaves **f, g, a, c** and **d** to choose from. Figure 4.9 shows the musical notation for this.

Figure 4.9   Pentatonic scale of **f**

On a glockenspiel the chosen notes are likely to be repeated at least once more. Pentatonic scales are devoid of harmonic tension and when used as a basis for improvisation, particularly with soft beaters and smooth rhythm patterns, they provide relaxing and captivating pieces of music.

Silence

Silence is a crucial aspect of music-making and a few moments of silence before and after a performance provides the perfect vessel to contain the music. The silence at the beginning provides the opportunity for the children to focus on what is about to happen and the final silence grants an instant to reflect and release any emotions created by the music. Silence is very difficult to achieve, however, by listening for it the children become aware of the ambience of the environment and any sound pollution it contains. Acoustic ambience is an important contributor to musical performance – a solo voice may be enhanced by an echoing environment, while a steel band would not. This contextual envelope into which music is placed forms part of the performance awareness the children should experience throughout their work. There are several electronic gadgets that enable reverberation and echo to be added to music and some music/CD players provide buttons designed to emulate differing levels of acoustical ambience.

Terms, phrases and expressions are an integral part of understanding music and are part of the normal expressive language related to the subject. Integral to engagement with the art form is the introduction and development of this language with the children.

Adagio for Strings – composed by Samuel Barber (1910–1981) – could be used as a starting point for studying slow music employing instruments with differing ranges but sharing a similar tonal quality. It could act as a springboard for children's own composition of an *Adagio for* ... Terms for speed, dynamics, instruments and types of composition all form a basis for this specialist language and should be taught within the context of a developmental programme.

RESPONSES TO MUSIC

Participation in music and its integration with other art forms provides a rich social environment for children. Performance and presentational work develops a close working relationship within the peer group. Often the artistic content is improved as the children foster a deeper understanding of each other's role within the music-making. A choral group, jazz ensemble or samba band are all examples of this level of social interaction. A collection of solo singers does not necessarily result in a good choir – the manner in which individuals work and blend together is vital.

Children are taught to listen, look and respond in a focused way as they acquire a variety of musical skills. Inclusion for all children is an imperative, and a perceived uniqueness of their role is highly desirable. Children are usually excited, motivated and stimulated by musical activities which also provide a way of reaching deeply into their psyche. Most children are highly responsive to these influences. Implicit in the programmes of study for music is a requirement to strike a balance between the children inventing their own music alongside playing music composed by others. These creative and re-creative aspects are different and complementary towards the children's overall musical development. In drama, this relates to devised or scripted pieces, where each has its own importance in providing additional experience for the children through which they achieve a deeper understanding of the art form. Interesting work can be achieved by children performing music devised by others in the same class or group.

USING THE MATERIALS OF MUSIC

The voice as a musical instrument presents activities that are immediately accessible to children. Vocal sounds, chants and songs provide building blocks for a variety of learning situations related to rhythm and pitch. The human voice possesses the capacity to evoke powerful moods and messages, and is the primary tool for projecting individual children into their broader surroundings. On a spoken level, modulation of the voice presents additional meaning and interest to the words. Altering the pitch or placing the voice in the throat, nasal cavities or chest is a way to depict different characters. Building words into cyclic patterns produces rhythm.

Young children often repeat words over and over to 'play with words' and the repetition can become quite hypnotic. Longer phrases can be used in a similar fashion to develop ritualistic chants or work rhythms hinged around a basic pulse. As children develop a sense of pulse every list of words, row of numbers and line in a book becomes the source of inspiration for rhythm work based around speech patterns. Conversely the words will gain a stronger significance by this treatment, and the partnership between words and rhythm will develop an appreciation of pattern, rhythmic memory and phrase.

Children develop a capacity for singing by the careful building of a repertoire related to themes, topics, projects, festivals and other performance work within the school calendar. Parallel to the relevance of the vocal repertoire comes the mechanics required to develop breath control, modulation, posture, projection, intonation, expression and phrasing as detailed in Chapter 2.

Extending rhythmic word patterns into percussion ostinati will present additional areas for the development of instruments. This can be placed within the context of accompaniment for songs, chants and movement as well as pure instrumental composition. Relationships of this nature form a natural part of an integrated teaching approach while developing the skills specifically related to pulse and rhythm. Figure 4.10 shows the way in which instrumental skills can be integrated into dance lessons. Providing children with access to a broad spectrum of instruments will extend their aural vocabulary and foster the thrill of sound, especially through sound combinations. An extensive sound vocabulary results in a higher potential for compositional ideas as well as stimulating memory and encouraging children to internalise sounds. Developing the ability to internalise and imagine musical sounds is a high order skill, which is an important part of musical development and should be actively encouraged. While following this route many children will encounter instruments they fall in love with – for some it will be a lifelong relationship while for others it will be a lifelong memory.

Figure 4.10 Group percussion accompaniment to dance

The relevance of all classroom instruments is encapsulated in their ability to provide access to music-making for the children, because, through them, the children learn, understand and develop musical skills by making music. Carl Orff (1895–1982) developed this practical approach to music education and his techniques still remain valid today. Tuned classroom percussion – chime bars, xylophones, metallophones and glockenspiels – are unique in their ability to facilitate the connections between melodies and harmonies in a concrete operational way. The simple methodology of being able to preselect the notes required for a chord or scale, while at the same time being aware of the letter names of the notes, is fundamental in developing an understanding of the development of pitch and harmony. These instruments also require a minimum of technique, so provide immediate access to the children. They also work well together and can be balanced in range, volume and timbre to achieve satisfying ensemble playing. Good supplies of beaters are required to access the full range of tonal quality available, particularly soft felt types for instruments in accompaniment roles.

Children develop a whole range of individual instrumental skills, both outside and within the school context, and it is imperative that these skills should be included within the class work and considered to be part of the same musical development. Various woodwind and brass instruments, as well as guitar and keyboard, remain popular. Children developing these specific instrumental skills will improve their playing by combining creative composition alongside the other techniques they develop during instrument lessons. Instrumental teachers are usually happy to assist with the inclusion of this specific instrumental work into the core of class music-making.

ICT provides children with many opportunities to access music-making, gives rapid access to information and provides the individual with final results which look and sound good. Consider a situation where children word process some of their written work, add a piece of clip art to illustrate the writing, use an art package to add their own drawings and then combine all these aspects into a desktop publishing presentation. This process, which is now very common practice, enhances the work beyond recognition. Equally, children could select different sounds and music from within the computer or Internet, add their own original work and manipulate it in a variety of ways to create their own pieces of music.

ICT is a valuable educative tool, currently developing rapidly in all areas of education with children gaining competence in its use and implementing the latest software. It is a powerful tool within music also, and must not be excluded. Children's compositions stay on file and are available to be played or combined with other work of a multimedia nature. Computers allow children to manipulate musical sounds. The speed, key or pitch of music can be changed and presented both in graphical form and established musical notation.

MOODS AND EMOTIONS

Expressing mood and emotions within music has been firmly on the agenda since the Romantic period of music. The nineteenth-century schools of composition lay claim to the idea but it must really have been in existence since the first mother sang to comfort her baby, and it has progressed to the level of becoming a constant companion to television programmes and films. Events, motion, locations, excitement and fear are all reliant upon the musical score to generate these feelings. This strand of musical technique provides many opportunities for the children to work in similar ways and engage with descriptive music. Work related to the sea can bring together:

- singing a sea shanty such as 'Haul Away Joe'
- listening and moving to sea music such as the overture to the *Flying Dutchman* by Richard Wagner (1813–1883)

- song based instrumental accompaniment work such as 'Sloop John B'
- compositional work such as rolling waves related to dynamics moving into a contrasting melodic section using lilting music in three time and extending the composition to relate with a story-line about lost treasure or pirates.

Such examples can only hint at the relationships the teacher and children will want to make. These will be established in their own particular ways and will be related to their chosen topics.

The discussion, planning and exploring will enable the children to capture a range of moods and emotions reflected in the way they employ the elements of music. Once the children are placed in controlled situations they will naturally create these effects in an intuitive way. The words 'mood' and 'emotion' can conjure heavy and psychological connotations. Musical 'essences' and 'flavours' are lighter substitutes for the same factors.

INTERPRETATION AND CONSTRUCTION OF MUSIC

Devising composition and developing presentational work fosters creativity within the children. Taking constituent parts and assembling them into a cohesive piece perpetually requires choice and decision-making skills to be employed. Listening and responding in a positive fashion are implicit for success. The art form also requires the development of these skills with ever-increasing levels of precision and accuracy. Integrated arts work encourages teachers and children to examine relationships that grow from artistic and non-artistic starting points in order to intensify the learning process. Fixed parameters, and other restrictive influences, often serve to encourage the most creatively fertile ground. Detailed analytical work, coupled to group and individual self-regulation, also form transferable skills developed by the children.

Not all music children create is sweet sounding, nor should it be. Some creations serve to illustrate frightening and ugly events, designed to fill the listener with fear and apprehension. It is important to ask the children to talk about their music, preferably before it is played, to become aware of the detail and also to discover particular listening points. A Key Stage 1 child selected a card picturing a fish and was required to choose an instrument that represented the animal. Small silver bells were selected and the child proceeded to play a quiet sound on the instrument. The relationship between the colour of the underside of the fish and the silvery finish of the bells was the reason for the choice. Another child played a guiro with a swishing action related to the way she imagined the fish was moving. Both are acceptable representations, which gain extra significance with the added knowledge of the stimulated imagination. All artistic attempts are acceptable within this early work and the appreciation of children's efforts encourages further attempts, in the same way that the acceptance of an idea from a child will encourage them to present more ideas. This can be a significant factor in developing confidence and positive self-image. All arts work provides opportunity for intellectual intrigue related to the artistic intention of the transmitter, the creator of the work, and the audience who are the receivers. Sometimes transmitted and received factors are wide apart, while in some instances they are obviously united.

THE REPERTOIRE OF MUSIC

Musical development conforms to the notion of a spiral curriculum where a known number of factors come round and round again. Each time children meet a factor, teachers seek to deepen and extend their knowledge, skill and understanding. Experience, confidence, independence, knowledge, maturation, established skills and gained understanding all have a bearing in the expected achievement. It is important to consider these factors to avoid repetition and to ensure that children make adequate progress throughout school life. Making high demands of an achievable nature is the teacher's aim along with the introduction of new skills and the teaching of techniques. In the first instance, teachers should present new skills and techniques to children and then allow them to be developed in their own way.

Throughout the primary school years, children gain an extensive repertoire of singing, progressively developing control over their voices as they acquire this repertoire. The development of singing skills will necessitate improvement in pitching notes, attention to diction, adding expression, controlling dynamics and establishing a level of independence in part singing. The song repertoire is likely to exceed 50, which will have integrated with all aspects of school life and curriculum. Quantity, quality and variety are important factors in the motivation of children, enabling them to control their vocal capacity in a practical sense. Style of language and the substance of the vocal material, appropriate to the age and maturity of the children, should also be considered. Songs will also require rehearsal to include expressive detail, unite the singers, aid concentration and improve focus. Teachers have plenty of scope in choosing vocal material to meet the needs of the children. There are many available lists of suggested ideas and materials to include in the repertoire, but a preferred option is the combination of the school's own devised material with that of others.

Accurate listening is crucial to musical development. Although children are very eager to participate, careful listening and the attendant mental processes often bring about increased levels of musical improvement. Recall, imagined/internalised performance and concentration form an important part of understanding and improving music. Listening to music performed by others establishes positive role models, stimulates ideas and also helps children and teachers to understand how to express ideas and feelings through music. Listening requires purpose and the development of vocabulary, coupled with language that permits the children to articulate their musical observations of both live and recorded music.

Closely related to listening is an understanding of the context in which music is placed. Experiencing different styles of event and occasion presents a valuable contribution to the curriculum, along with the variety of musical genres represented in performances. Culture and history form additional contextual areas of knowledge. Through an understanding of these fields children become aware of the expressive language through which they can subsequently respond, react and analyse music. Children should be furnished with situations that promote discussion, reflection, adjustment and general educated comment related to their musical experiences.

Playing percussion instruments is specifically related to encouraging creativity and the development process involved in composition. Manual dexterity and hand–eye coordination contribute to the progression of this work and enable the children to increase their levels of sophistication. Making instrumental choices and organising sounds into a musical composition is a problem-solving technique required by all composers, which then develops into the combination of sounds with added form and structure. Positive reinforcement and fun will assist the children to devise simple repeating musical patterns, which progress through a period of time to enhance melodic and rhythmic senses.

The perfect piece of music has yet to be composed, hence the need to teach analytical skills which will assist the children to improve their work. Open-ended questions, designed to motivate lateral thinking, will assist the young composers to make improvements to their work and can assist them to achieve a required effect, mood or style. A variety of activities will enable children to accomplish the skills of modification and appraisal within individual and corporate contexts.

What if ...?
Have you thought about ...?
How about trying ...?
How about changing ...?

The outcome of such exercises will be presented in the form of music that is closer to perfection. Rote, routine and rehearsal are intrinsic aspects of music–making that improve the quality of performance – well planned rehearsals always result in improved performances.

Memorising musical improvisation and using aides-mémoire is the accepted technique for recreating children's work at Key Stage 1. Invented signs and symbols are progressively introduced to extend the musical memory while maintaining order and structure. Any notational invention requires interpretation for the performers and standard notation is no exception to this. Because conventional notation is a standard it is impossible to avoid its presence, however, it is merely a means to an end and not an end in itself. Within this context sections of standard notation could well be used within, or combined with, graphical scores. Sign and symbols are used to represent systems designed to indicate what is happening and when it happens, representing an order in place and time.

Children's musical development is tempered with a breadth of study that combines a range of activities designed to integrate performing, composing and the ability to make qualitative judgements about musical activities. The content potential is vast and teachers will be faced with making professional judgements related to time, quality and quantity. Integration with other art forms and subject areas will assist in maintaining a strong provision in music and contextualise it within a broader knowledge base.

CREATING THE MUSICAL ENVIRONMENT AND EXTENDING CRITICAL AWARENESS

Adequate resources will be required and they should include sufficient sound producers to interest and motivate the children. Such a collection will include tuned and untuned classroom percussion instruments, orchestral instruments, world instruments, ICT sound sources, body sounds, junk instruments and voices. Through these means, children build up their critical and conceptual powers of music.

It is important to provide a wide choice of musical sound sources for the children to facilitate greater opportunities in exploration and individual development. Sound producers that represent a variety of ethnic backgrounds and reflect differing musical genres will broaden the children's experiences. Children are often stimulated by the desire to play a particular instrument and are highly motivated by the opportunities presented for them to do so. A wide choice, coupled with situations which present the chance to exert choice, is essential.

The selection and availability of recorded music has never been greater. The high street music shop provides well catalogued music from historical periods, styles and types, compilation samplers and music from across the world. Most teachers are already working in a relatively rich audio environment, however, technology is moving apace, providing even greater advancements and impacting on children. Interactive technology already provides CDs that not only reproduce the music on a CD player but also allow the user to put the same disc into a PC and follow the musical score on screen, read about the composers, artist and their works and print hard-copy information.

The Internet is a vast source of information and teaching materials from across the world. Midi (musical instrument digital interface) files of thousands of pieces of music are available for downloading and are a particularly useful source for songs. The appropriate software enables a midi file to be played, edited and/or printed out for musical parts. Part of this editing process allows for the removal of tunes, repeating of sections, removal of sections and so on.

Flexibility will be required in meeting the variety of ways music resources are used and made available to children. A classroom based exercise requires the availability of equipment in that area, while at other times the work is taking place in the hall or other large area suitable for combining with dance or drama. Figure 4.11 shows a child playing an instrument as an accompaniment to work in dance. Specialist rooms also figure in this equation. The children require access to resources in all these different locations which are dependent on the context of their work. One special area of the school requires to be established as the music base, where displays, books of reference, instruments and recordings can live tidily. Although equipment will be perpetually moving about the school, the children must be taught to handle instruments with care and respect. Repair or discard broken instruments quickly and make sure everything is fresh and clean.

Figure 4.11   Integrating sound and movement

THE CULTURAL CONTEXT OF MUSIC

The wide range of media resources currently available provides numerous opportunities for teachers and children to investigate cultural aspects of music and to integrate them with practical experiences. The following account is an exemplar of a how one particular school made music special.

A multicultural approach

This example of a school integrated arts project provides a series of topic ideas and how they relate to the resultant performance experience for children at Key Stage 2. Groups of children from each class within the school embarked upon music-topic based work related to different parts of the world with extension ideas into different curriculum subjects. The core of their work involved the planning, creating and development of the following themes.

Class 3,1 (Year 3)

The whole class listened to Chinese music played on the shakuhachi (bamboo flute) and the children were taught a Chinese ribbon dance using prerecorded music. The dance involved a fixed series of steps with stylised shapes and patterns. Colourful ribbons were used as extensions to the arm and hand movements. The basic ribbon costumes used ribbon about the waist and as cross-sashes. The dance work was instigated by a one-day input from a Chinese dancer and developed by the class teacher.

Classes 4,1 and 4,2 (Year 4)

The first class worked in groups using untuned Chinese musical instruments – gongs, cymbals and drums. The drum held a steady pulse related to the speed of a dragon moving. Gongs played a series of rapid strokes at twice the speed of the pulse. This produced an impressive wall of sound that gradually built in energy and volume. Cymbals played single and double beats related to the gesture of the dragon's head and added vigour and drama to the music. Three-dimensional art work produced two large dragon heads with fabric bodies which went on to be used for a dragon dance. The music and movement were combined to form a short theatrical piece.

The second class worked on a musical improvisation constructed around a series of events based on the Chinese dragon: waking up, walking, dancing, shaking and falling asleep. The focus of the improvisations was to depict the series of events in a story-line, which makes it possible to employ a broad range of instruments alongside those from the specific culture. Waking up and falling asleep were based on the use of dynamics while walking and dancing made use of regular pulse work. Dancing further combined the use of layered melodic lines based on a pentatonic scale and performed on tuned percussion instruments. This large group of children was less experienced at using musical instruments and their work involved very high degrees of involvement and freedom. Cards were produced with the key word titles of each section. Smaller writing and signs were added around the key word as reminders of the content of each piece. The cards were then used as a simple score. Each improvisation diminished in volume as the card disappeared from view, prompting a moment of silence before the next section began.

The Chinese cultural elements extended further into the curriculum for all three classes in Years 3 and 4 to include the Chinese calendar, customs and foods.

Class 5,1 (Year 5)

Asian stick dancing accompanied by singing and rhythmic instrumental playing was at the hub of work based on Diwali as a theme. The children learned actions for the stick dance, and a second group worked out a rhythmic collage using dollaks and bells. The stick dance was a repeating pattern established by clicking sticks together at knee, waist, chest and head heights. The second section of the dance involved clicking by the chest and then with stick to stick of a partner repeated four times over. Sticks for the dance were cut and decorated by the children.

Class 6,1 (Year 6)

This class learned native African music by using a selection of drums including a talking drum and two African thumb pianos (kalimbas). The music was based on layered ostinati with each instrument entering in turn to build upon a steady pulse played throughout on a bass drum made from a plastic bin. Each ostinati was equated to a rhythmic speech pattern repeated over and over. Once the rhythms were fixed the order of each part entering was decided and kept constant. The instrumental work introduced the reading of an African story, *Bringing the Rain to Kapiti Plain*, and scenes from the story were acted out by some of the children.

Whole-school performances

Each class had a number of display areas related to their topic containing books, musical instruments, clothes, fabrics, pictures and accounts written by the children. A professional artist provided a banner-painting workshop and the children produced four large banners to hang in the school hall representing different facets of the theme. The whole school learned a collection of Christmas songs and carols.

The project ran throughout the autumn term and culminated in a celebratory performance at the end of term. Classes presented their work to a capacity audience of parents and friends in the school hall as the first stage of the Midwinter Celebration. Stage two was a street procession which transported all the children and their audience to the church and included elements of each of the class performances: ribbon dancers, dragons, stick dancers, Asian and African drummers combining into a samba band, banner carriers plus a small imported brass ensemble of comprehensive school children bringing up the rear. The procession, complete with police escort, journeyed its exuberant way through the streets of the estate until it reached the local church. Once inside the church the celebration concluded with a modern interpretation of the nativity story, punctuated with Christmas carols and songs accompanied by guitar, piano, piano accordion, pipe organ, recorders and percussion instruments. The songs chosen represented a variety of styles to include gospel, rock, reggae and Latin types. Each section of the performance lasted approximately 40 minutes and extended the work into a community project focused on the achievements of the school.

Extensive resources exist within the broader community which can be integrated into the curriculum in order to enrich the experiences of the children and extend the resources available to the teacher. Although it is not necessary for projects to be carried out on this large scale, it does serve as a reminder of the importance of the arts in enhancing the profile, ethos and image of a school and projecting positive images of its pupils.

THE PIVOTAL ROLE OF MUSIC IN RELATION TO DRAMA, DANCE AND ART

Figure 4.12 illustrates the pivotal relationship between the integrated arts viewed from the perspective of music. The musical skills and language, as the music mode of communication, embrace the main route of learning from the Reception class and through the programme of study at Key Stages 1 and 2. The experiences the children receive can link to their studies in drama via the use of recordings – perhaps as scratch music compiled from diverse sound sources or as anthologies of sound using conventional instruments. There are extensive opportunities to implement the learning experiences advocated in this chapter within the realms of drama, and incorporating stories and poems.

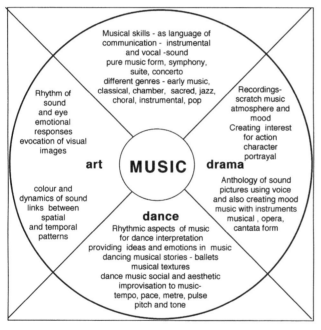

Figure 4.12   The pivotal role of music

There has always been a close, and in some instances indivisible, relationship between music and dance, and links occur at historical, multicultural and technical levels. The elements of music, its basic expressive language, link with those of dance so that high and low sounds and movements match, rhythm corresponds, and the melodic line or texture of sound is mutually conveyed. There is a wide range of musical received works available that children enjoy listening to and using for dance improvisation and composition. In visual art there are semblances, and opportunities exist for mutual collaboration, especially through the evocation of mood and visual composition. Music creates an environment of sound, the elements of which relate to those of vision. The sense of rhythm, melody, pitch, volume and musical dynamic – elements that create the mood of music – correspond with the rhythm, colour, eye patterns and relationships within a painting or within sculpture. Understanding about how ideas and feelings are conveyed visually can be used to understand about how ideas and feelings are conveyed musically. Transposition also occurs through the images that sounds induce, so aesthetically there is a highly sensitive relationship between music and art – a thematic teaching approach draws out this understanding. For example, listening to the storm scene from the overture of *Peter Grimes* by Benjamin Britten (1913–1976) will conjure up images that reflect the rhythm, colour and tone of the music and will contrast with the imagery of the sea that can be induced by listening to *La Mer* by Claude Debussey (1862–1918).

PERSONAL COLLECTION OF COMPOSITIONS AND EXPERIENCES

Music is a time based art form and is quite illusive in nature. Good work cannot always be mounted on the wall for all to see. Performance to others does allow the work to receive acclimation and presents an additional dynamic which can be both positive and negative due to the difference in emotional dynamics. Audio and/or video recording should become customary practice along with personal computer files, logbooks of musical experiences and workbooks. These different techniques will assist in freezing musical moments in time or present opportunities to re-create a new experience based on work from the past.

When a child or group of children have recorded their music the recording can be used to accompany dance, drama or an art and design installation.

PERFORMANCE

Live performance is an important part of developing musical interest. The children will be performing to each other and to others in the broader school community. Visits to performances are often inspirational to the children and enhance the quality of their work. Performers who visit the school can also make a valuable contribution to role modelling. Musicians from the local secondary school, parents, friends and colleagues who play instruments, youth groups and community bands – all have a contribution to make in providing live music experiences.

Professional artists are keen to work with young people and there are schemes available to assist with financing such projects. The experience children gain from a live perform-ance is often intense and evocative of long-term positive memories. This intensity is unique and should be an integral part of the creative arts curriculum available to the children. Visual artists, dancers and actors also present the same opportunities for the children. Many of these artistic visitors exhibit high degrees of dedication and enthusi-asm, which is detected by the children and enhances the contagious qualities present within the arts.

The recording and reporting of musical experiences with children will follow the same format as presented in the two previous chapters on dance and drama, but placing the criteria for judgement within a musical framework, so that doing and listening become the key experiences as expressed through:

- the children's operational skills of music-making
- the children's achievements in musical presentations

- the children's critical understanding of the processes in making music
- the children's understanding of the cultural background to their own musical experiences.

Children's music-making and appreciation is greatly enhanced by the use of new technologies.

ICT IN MUSIC

Access to information has been revolutionised by computer technology and development of the Internet. Children will continue to develop skills that will assist them in finding and processing good information from the ever-increasing library of knowledge. The multimedia style of this information is presented as music, pictures, articles and video. Detailed information can be obtained relating to composers, instruments, cultures, genres, concerts, plays, dance companies, arts projects and events. The revolutionary aspect relates to the immediacy and quality of this information. Technology is the gatekeeper of this knowledge and its contributors are positioned across the globe. Huge selections of information are available for researching any subject, project or topic. ICT is a powerful and necessary tool for the children which both enhances and informs their music, whether as creators, performers or as investigators. Recordings of music can be exchanged between children from school to school across the world, other people's opinions sought and specialist knowledge provided.

Interactive CDs provide additional reference resources with encyclopaedias that quickly search related topics and assist in placing information in historical and geographical contexts.

CHAPTER 5

The Visual Art Mode

Music, drama and dance are arts that express themselves from within the creative self and, as part of an integrated arts mode, conjoin with visual art which is an external representation since the art object is created in material form. Painting and sculpture are fine art forms which are symbolic representations of ideas whereas the functional forms of art are evident in architecture and the arts of design. Art is fashioned from world resources, and the natural environment has provided the stimulus for wide-ranging art activities both as the stimulus for design and in the way in which the properties of its materials has determined the form of the art object. Civilisations have each left their mark. The diverse range of architectural forms and artifacts provide clues to belief and value systems that transcend geographical and historical boundaries. World cultures – once unknown, exclusive or inaccessible – have revealed their secrets and provided rich sources of interest. Architecture, whether on a grand scale or domestic and vernacular, has provided the enclosure or hearth in which the day-to-day living activities have taken place. Body adornment, clothing, jewellery, furniture, cooking vessels and eating utensils have been crafted over generations, with new techniques and new materials superseding previous ones and past styles influencing the latest designs and creations.

The evolutionary and revolutionary changes of the world brought about by discovery, invention and new technologies has impacted upon the way people live, the style of their homes, the clothes they wear, the products they use, and the places of artistic interest they visit and where they have chosen to display their objects of cultural heritage. Reference points for the study and celebration of large- or small-scale art can be found throughout the world where there are fine examples of decorative art, often reflecting geographical and sociological conditions. Carvings, architectural embellishments, sculptures, tapestries, ceramic tiles, pewter and copper ware, are art objects of home and hearth. In European cultures, royal palaces, cathedrals, churches and the domestic habitat were the places to display fine art, paintings, sculptures or portraits. Examples of artifacts from Japan, China, Indonesia, the Orient, the Middle East, the Far East, North America, South America, Africa and Australasia can be viewed in national collections supported by published secondary and Internet sources. The way in which teachers are able to access and select examples from this rich and diverse resource influences the quality of the art experience their pupils receive.

Children's understanding of the visual world starts with home, their immediate daily surroundings, and school. They become familiar with materials and utensils – toys, picture books, the layout of their bedroom, patterns of wallpaper and curtains, and the changing scenes they view on television. Children absorb the visual shape of their environment with its vibrant colours, its shadows and its highlights and images and pictures become organised within their mind. They recognise and recall the changing scenes of their life and both vivid and hazy images enter their minds. The real world can be consciously envisaged. By closing their eyes the children can conjure up a picture of the classroom or the journey to school. They identify buildings, trees, roads, pavements, shops. Images also enter into the subconscious mind and surface in dreams or are transformed into childhood fantasies.

Children adjust and react to their immediate environment. In the same manner that their responses lead to dances, plays and music which capture their feelings and their thinking, so too, children are able to convey their thoughts and feeling in their art work. Seeing comes before speaking, and together with movement and tactile feeling, represents the way in which children perceive the world. The way in which visual perception is ultimately processed is closely linked with the development of creativity and skill that leads to the production of an artifact. This can be through two-dimensional mark-making as in drawing and painting or using three-dimensional form, such as clay.

At school, the classroom becomes the window on the world, supplemented with the latest technology and enhanced through using the resources of museums and art galleries. Children learn about the art of past generations and other cultures. The relationship between what children know, understand and express in their own art work is comprehended in the context of what other artists and crafts people have understood and conveyed by way of their art work. The most powerful way of helping children to comprehend the work of other artists is through their own practical experiences of art-making, and conversely, a way of helping children to understand their own art work is through knowing about the received works of the world.

Introducing children to art commences at the preschool stage. A good nursery school or playgroup relies a great deal on providing practical experiences of paint, clay, crayon, pencil, dough, fabrics and recycled materials for children's early stages of art. Often when children are permitted to come to terms with different materials gained through their own innate curiosity, they are able to develop their own creative skills. High standards of achievement will only be obtained when children work with media that enhances rather than inhibits powers of expression and communication. It is important that teachers recognise the appropriate use of materials and ideas that correspond with children's development and understanding of the nature of visual art as they progress through the primary stages. The use of a range of materials and a variety of art-making processes allows for a great wealth of experience, as well as demanding the mastery of a number of skills. Primary school children enjoy painting, building up a montage or collage, and constructing a three-dimensional sculpture. They also gain satisfaction through the manipulation and exploration of shape and texture derived from the use of clay, sand, and wood.

As in other modes of learning, children pass through observable stages starting with the exploratory experiences of the infant with intense curiosity and avid investigation directed towards the manipulation and shaping of ideas from the material source. The tension and effort of children experimenting with a different material enables them to discover its true nature so that they can fashion their ideas from it. The second stage becomes more relaxed and pleasurable, with some inner force that links material, idea and outcome. When left undisturbed with a carefully selected material, perhaps following discussion, children come to know and enjoy its properties and through experimentation are able to create with materials in a way that is meaningful and productive. At Reception and Key Stage 1 the imposition of adult ideas will inevitably inhibit, or even destroy the ability to communicate creatively. Instead the teacher assumes a role that befits the needs of the children – enabling, suggesting, demonstrating, discussing, guiding, instructing – whichever is appropriate in order to allow children to make progress through personal decision-making.

THE TEACHING AND LEARNING FRAMEWORK FOR VISUAL ART AND DESIGN

In experiencing the artistic process in school, children are not only being encouraged to develop and express their own creativity, but are also being prepared to become the critical receivers of the works of others. In the visual arts, this means opening up the possibilities in the school and making use of opportunities within the community and the locality – nationally and internationally – in order to celebrate and access the selected aspects of the world's cultural heritage. To enrich the child's own creative experience and to introduce and develop a broader cultural understanding of art, examples of art works, visits, displays and access to books are required. This entails formulating and adhering to school policy on resourcing as well as utilising support agencies and services, including artists in education, the showing of films and slides, computer technology, and involving children in arts projects. The programme for visual art and design is enhanced by the experiences of the performing arts and is grouped around the four areas of study as follows:

- participation in art – children's practical knowledge of art-making
- collection of art – children's portfolio of their own art works
- critical skills of art – children's knowledge of the qualities of art experienced through their own art-making and viewing artifacts of others expressed through discussion and writing
- context of art – children's knowledge of the historical, social and cultural worlds that have inspired or informed their understanding of art.

A diagrammatic representation is shown in Figure 5.1.

PARTICIPATION IN ART

The activity of art-making through personal engagement allows children to acquire a number of visual and manual skills through using a range of materials and media in two- or three-dimensional forms. Practical art work will include: drawing, painting, printing, dyeing, collage, modelling, construction, sculpture, textiles, mixed media and digital art. Children learn to understand the properties of the materials they are using, acquire the skills of manipulation and dexterity, and relate these skills to a desired effect through a series of problem formulation and solution-seeking stages in order that the process of art will lead to a finished result. This will involve working individually and working with a partner or in small groups.

Participation	Repertoire
Acquiring skills:	Acquiring a collection of artifacts through:
• visual and manual skills	• drawings in sketchbooks
• skills of wide range of materials and media	• portfolio of own works
• problem-solving skills	• work displayed in classroom and school
• formulating ideas	• painting and printing
• through materials and media to create artifacts	• puppets and masks
• 2D and 3D forms	• murals and classroom environments

VISUAL ART

Context	Critical awareness
Discovering about visual art and design:	Discussion and writing about the experiences of art-making:
• visits to galleries	• as self-analysis
• reference books and stories about art and artists	• as viewer of art of peers
• designers and crafts persons	• as visitor to gallery and exhibitions
• use of ICT	• as reader of books on art and design
• professional artists in school	• developing a metalanguage to discuss the experiences of visual art and design

Figure 5.1 A framework for the teaching and learning of visual art

In the first instance children, supported by their teachers, will grapple with ideas, materials and processes, adapting and adjusting according to circumstance in order to bring about a resolution. This is based on the harmonious relationship between:

• the child's own artistic idea – what is envisaged
• the way in which the child understands the working of the material
• the way in which the child develops the skill in using the material
• the interaction of the teacher in developing individual percipience.

Drawing is the underlying fundamental art activity that supports all other forms of artistic engagement, since it prepares children to be detailed and specific about recording what they see and what they imagine. Children's drawings are their individual and unique commentaries of the visual world. The content and the subject of drawings, by their arrangement in relation to each other and in the density or fineness of line, provides a commentary or description. This is expressed according to individual levels of artistic accomplishment, and not least by children's ability to master the skills required of the mark-making instrument. Chalks, pastel, crayon, charcoal and pencil not only offer young children the most direct and accessible means of giving form to their perceptions, feelings and ideas, they are the instruments through which they acquire their vocabulary of artistic form.

Comprehending how marks, shapes and patterns on paper represent either the visible, tangible world, or the pictures in the child's own mind, is the first stage of grasping the significance and purpose of art. Aesthetic feelings associated with the process of art-making are awakened through drawing. These include the major areas of observational

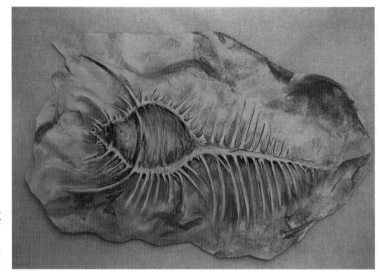

Figure 5.2 Drawing – the basis of all forms of artistic engagement. Study by a student teacher of a sea shell

drawing, recalling from memory and inventing from the imagination. Figure 5.2 is a large-scale investigative study of a sea shell, drawn in pastel, by a student teacher.

Children's experience of painting, although supported by their drawing and other forms of visual investigation recorded in sketchbooks, is based upon how they learn to work in this medium, which has its own special properties. The handling skills of working correctly with tools and implements is obviously related to the nature of the materials being used. Making and using printing blocks and applying printing inks also demands a specific medium based response, so that the properties of printing on paper, or printing on fabrics are experienced and understood. The use of fabric and textiles will require children to develop a number of skills in a safe way – dyeing fabrics, cutting, sewing, weaving and selecting and applying beads, sequins or braid – in order to create a wide variety of different artifacts ranging from wall hangings to soft sculptures. Basic skill requirements for collage are cutting, tearing, pasting and sticking, but the organisation of a collage, its design, arrangement of the materials, colours and textures draw upon other more complex aspects of artistry.

Three-dimensional work in the primary school focuses on aspects of modelling, whether using clay or plasticine, or construction sculpture which uses boxes, wood, wire, papier mâché and mod-rock. Mixed media, when children can select and use a combination of visual art forms, is to be encouraged. Experimental time devoted to producing ideas from the materials is a worthwhile and necessary stage. The computer can be used as a process instrument for design purposes, or as an art medium in its own right.

Experimenting with a range of two- and three-dimensional materials such as paper, card, cloth, wood, clay, plaster, soap, colouring agents and adhesives leads to the production of paintings, collage, montage, box sculpture, models and constructions. Clay work includes thumb work, coil, slab, moulding and surface treatments. Textiles include printing, appliqué, tie-and-dye, embroidery and making puppets – whether finger, sock, glove, shadow, string, or giant puppets for use in the playground. Scale and usage need to be taken into account, but as well as pure art, simple theatre and drama costumes and properties can be manufactured.

A PERSONAL PORTFOLIO OR COLLECTION

Evidence of children's understanding in art at each specific stage of their development is revealed in the personal collection of art works that they have produced as they progress through the primary school. Throughout the school day, both inside and outside of art lessons, children make drawings and graphic representations of their ideas. They decorate borders and margins surrounding their writing tasks, they illustrate humanity lessons by drawing maps, diagrams, facsimiles and scenes of past events. Design skills are used in science and technology. Continuing use of sketchbooks, and building up an individual folder or portfolio of children's work supports and values independent endeavour. Additionally, over the academic year, the teacher will build up a class collection of work, some of which will have been part of displays in school or exhibited within the local community, photographed or video-recorded.

Collaborative and individual children's work forms the collection of artifacts which include examples of paintings, prints, models, sculptures, puppets, masks and pottery. The themes and ideas that have stimulated visual art work relate to those that have inspired and informed work in dance, drama and music, and encompasses: abstract art forms, representational art, functional art, surrealistic art, literary art and designing and making for the performance arts. Children's abstract art is characterised by patterns and designs that have been generated from the use of line, geometrical forms or colour. Abstract art, being non-literal and non-representative of nature or the surrounding visual world, allows for the free invention of design. As in dance choreography, spatial significance is created through relationships of straight, angular and curved lines, volume and density implied through the arrangement of the elements within the picture. Establishing a particular motif, which may form a theme and variation or be recurring, will give each piece of work its individual identity. Specific design motifs or schemata characterise stages in children's artistic awareness, from free-form scribble to discernible spirals, concentric circles and rectilinear patterns.

Children's representational drawings, paintings or sculptural models reflect the world realistically as a 'faithful copy' of nature, portraying that which is seen in a style and manner unique to that child. It can include the drawing and painting of trees, flowers, fruit and plants, as well as buildings, the interior of rooms, or children playing. The teacher may have taken the children on a visit, or outside school, or the scenes may have been composed from memory or using the imagination. Representational art also includes recording still-life inanimate objects made from wood, stone, glass, metal and fabric. Children's toys, kitchen objects, machine parts, bicycles and historical artifacts all hold a special fascination.

Children's experience of functional art is through design tasks that relate to purposeful objects in life. Designing for living helps children to become aware of the role of art in everyday life and, specifically, their own lives. Houses and homes, transport, clothing, furnishings, wallpaper, carpet and furniture, especially when resourced from a historical and future time perspective, is a stimulating and important experience that allows the new generation to discover its own dominant style.

In contrast, surrealistic art allows the children to enjoy the powers of their own imagination, dreaming up images and finding a super reality. Inspired by science fiction, films, listening to music or reading poetry, children invent their own bizarre artifacts. The experimental use of media will include the irrational juxtaposition of images.

Literary art refers to children's art work created from the direct inspiration of poems or stories. Children's own book illustrations are one of the most enjoyable forms of art appreciation, aiding their own reading and enjoyment of texts. Similarly, illustrations of their own writing, whether fiction or non-fiction, in big books or as a class magazine or newspaper produced on the computer, are a valid form of artistic expression.

Designing and making for the performance arts will include different sorts of masks and puppets as well as costume and scenic effects. It includes finger, glove, and stick puppets, and giant puppets, simple puppet theatres, box constructions for classroom environments, and items as historical artifacts or drama properties.

CRITICAL AWARENESS

From early explorations of mark-making to the development of artistry, children's own understanding of their art-making develops when teachers actively encourage understanding of the art process and the nature of the work produced by implementing a number of strategies. These will take the form of interactive discussion:

- at the start of the lesson when new ideas are being introduced and new skills demonstrated
- during the lesson when children are in the process of art-making
- when the work has been completed.

From the outset, children are encouraged to ask and answer questions about the starting points for their work, and to comment as they develop their ideas. Reviewing work is an important factor for understanding the art process and its impact on final results. The interactive discussion can be extended by incorporating points of reference to specific examples of the work of artists, crafts people and designers. There will be resources available for this purpose. The development of talk, acquiring and using a metalanguage can be further developed through written work and incorporated within literacy.

CULTURAL CONTEXT

The vibrancy of children's own art work is enhanced when they become sensitively aware and appreciative of other works of art that somehow relate to their own work and will be linked to what is known about selected historical, social, cultural, philosophical, or aesthetic aspects of painting, sculpture, architecture, industrial design or photography. School policies and individual teachers are most successful when they focus on select examples from the world of art which can be brought into the lives of the children by means of appropriate and obtainable resources:

- authentic art brought into the school
- reproduction art within the school
- authentic art visited in the locality housed in museums and galleries
- authentic art visited nationally
- use of published and media resources including ICT.

At Reception and Key Stage 1 it is required that children see examples of craft and design from the community and from different times and cultures. These experiences are developed at Key Stage 2 when children are able to investigate the different types of roles played by artists, crafts people and designers, by examining their work in the community or taking examples from different times and cultures. Approaches towards building up a meaningful programme for children entails examining how to access the best of the available facilities, and how these fit in and complement the planned curriculum. It requires a concerted effort of sharing expertise and experience with some allocation of investment within each school.

Ideally, the school will build up a collection of resources to be shared that include examples of artifacts crafted from wood, metal, and clay, with examples of weaving, whether carpets, wall hangings or baskets. Some examples will be authentic, others reproduction items, and will also include examples of the craft work of India, South America and Africa which are readily obtainable along with Chinese porcelain and ornaments. In some areas it is possible to loan items. Resources emanating from the community will depend on the following factors:

- the visual resources of the local environment within walking distance – townscape, landscape, the street, immediate architectural features of buildings
- the nearest buildings of architectural interest within a short journey and with access to the interior – church, chapel, factory, vernacular architecture of street, housing estate etc.
- special short-journey excursions – to a museum, art gallery, library, heritage site
- human resources in the form of artists and museum education officers who come into school.

Careful consideration of the use of resources in art will complement the creative, contextual and critical experiences in the performing arts. Gaining knowledge of materials and the basic terminology of such aspects as tone, colour, texture, contrast, balance, focus, proportion, line and the way in which visual symbols are used to convey ideas and feeling are necessary attributes. This knowledge derives from personal powers of observing and describing, an awareness of design and the relationship of form and function, and a knowledge of styles, including the richness of different cultural forms. This broadly refers to Western, Oriental, African and American, and will include early forms of art, ancient (including Greek and Roman), medieval, Renaissance, baroque, neo-classical and modern. Handling and exploiting materials, and the acquisition of the appropriate skills would indicate work in the interrelated areas of drawing, painting, printing and various forms of three-dimensional construction work.

INSTRUMENTAL USE OF MATERIALS AND MEDIA

Children investigating and making in art, craft and design learn to use a range of materials and processes involving different tools and techniques. Practical experiences in visual art, craft and design focus on the creative and technical skills in a number of areas which can be integrated with the performance arts as well as being free standing. Fundamental to this is the ability to draw, since children create their own unique structural principles that make the meaning and content of their drawings understood. Mark-making is determined by the material used, so offer graphite sticks, sketch sticks, charcoal, pencils, sketch pens, microliners, stick pens, felt-tip pens, colour pencils, brush pens and ball-point pens. Children at Key Stage 2 also enjoy drawing inks.

Pencils range from the very fine F through to H, HB and B. The range B, with numbers from 2 to 8, is the best for drawing because it is soft. Pencil crayons give a good line and gentle colour. Children discover and enjoy the properties of charcoal, which is soft, distinctive to handle and highly effective. Highlights can be achieved either by rubbing out or overlaying with white chalk. Coloured chalks or pastels can add interesting effects, as can pasting tissue paper onto sugar paper to make an interesting background. Conte crayon is similar in texture to charcoal but is available in a number of colours – brown, black, grey, white and terracotta. The sticks can make sharp lines giving good definition. Chalk pastels are available in a variety of colours, and like charcoal and conte crayon, can be blended and smudged to create interesting effects and depth. Oil pastels have a different base, and this means there is a greater definition. They glide across the paper and colours will overlay, but they will not smudge or blend with ease.

Crayons, whether fluorescent, metallic or plastic, are made in different sizes ranging from chubby stumps for tiny hands to grasp to fine wax crayons. They are used for drawings and rubbings over different textures, for example, bark, brick, stone and flooring. White wax candle rubbed over paper forms the background of wax-resistant pictures or patterns. Pastels and the colour sticks are useful when ultra-sensitive work is demanded and are most effective when applied to coloured paper. 'Sgraffito' is the scratching through of a design or picture on a scraper board or made-up equivalent. Remember the significance of keeping personal sketchbooks or compiling class sketchbooks from loose leaves. Children delight in sketching people, other children, plants, animals and objects in the room.

Throughout the twentieth century numerous artists have used and developed drawing, providing a variety of style, subject and technique. Works by Picasso (1881–1973), Matisse (1869–1954), Miró (1893–1983), Stella (1936–), and David Hockney (1937–) reflect the diversity and range of drawing and go beyond Paul Klee's (1879–1940) description of taking a line for a walk. Digital media has opened up a new dimension for children, giving both confidence and enjoyment.

Alongside drawing is the experience of painting. A simple definition of painting is the art of representing or depicting by colours on a surface. Colour can be defined as being the tints and hues that are put into a picture, which may represent those observed in nature or images occurring within the imagination. Pigments are the paints or dyes as dry substances which, when mixed with a liquid substance, provide the medium with which to paint. The preferred paint in primary schools is powder colour as it is versatile, economical and easy to use. It is water-soluble but can be mixed with other binders. Good quality powder paint will not become chalky or muddy with use but will retain brilliance whether used as a thick paste or a thin wash. Learning to see colour and to understand its terminology is vital to its use. The emotional aspects of colour relate to the painter as much as to the observer, so it is important that children are able to mix the paints to the colour of their requirement.

In painting colour can be described using various terms, each with their specific meaning. For example:

- Hue is colour – for example, red, green or blue etc.
- Shade is the gradation of darkness and depth of a hue.
- Tint is the gradation of lightness.
- Tone is the overall effect of light and shade.
- All colours have a degree of brilliance.
- The primary colours are red, yellow and blue.
- The secondary colours are orange, green and violet and they can be achieved by mixing two primary colours together, gradually adding small amounts of each colour at a time until the correct hue appears which marks halfway between the two primary colours (red and yellow make orange, blue and yellow make green and red and blue make purple).
- The tertiary colours are made up by mixing a primary colour with a secondary colour, and are red-orange, yellow-orange, blue-green, yellow-green, blue-violet and red-violet.
- The colour wheel is based on the concept of a circle, which reading clockwise registers yellow, orange, red, violet, blue and green.

In addition to powder paints, colour blocks, ready-mixed paints, finger paints, poster paints, glitter paint and metallic powder paint are available. Children learn to mix their paints to determine the final effect. Offer children a selection of brushes to use, either large round-headed, broad-headed or flat or fine pointed, chosen according to need (perhaps determined by the size of the work or the type of paint and paper being used). Useful sizes are 6, 8 and 10, with fine detail of 4 and 6. These include pure sable, hog's hair, imitation sable, fine-point white nylon and ox-hair.

Printing and dyeing, using paper and fabrics are essential experiences in art. Block printing is appropriate for the primary school child and printing blocks can be made from polystyrene. Safety is an important factor and lino-printing, which requires the use of cutters, is best restricted to work at Key Stage 2 level. Handicraft printing inks are viscous, water based colours that are easily cleaned by washing in water. Available in large tubes specially for the purpose, it is also possible to use ready-mixed paint and powder paint, especially if thickened with a safe adhesive or paste. The consistency must be thick, but spread in such a way that it will not bleed into the design image.

Fabric paints can be mixed to obtain a variety of colours. The trays must be flat-bottomed and the ink is then rolled out using rubber rollers. Always start by squeezing a strip of ink along one end of the tray, or a series of shorter lengths of different colours. Roll ink down the tray and then diagonally from corner to corner, horizontally across, and vertically upwards to ensure even distribution. After creating a design motif on paper, draw it quite deeply into the polystyrene block or cut out some shapes. Roll or colour over and then press onto the paper, rolling over with a rolling pin or clean roller. Repeat the process, building up a design plan.

Printing techniques can be used individually or in combination with other printing techniques and/or mixed media. Natural materials, such as leaves, seed heads, tree bark, feathers, shells and stones can each be used as printing implements. Sponge printing is effective, especially when used as a background for other types of detail. Children can make their own printing block from cardboard cut-outs which they then glue down. Mono printing is when the ink is rolled out evenly in a tray and then a pattern is drawn into the ink with a pencil. Children press the paper into the ink and peel it away very carefully, as shown in the prints made by Hannah and Lauretta, based on natural formations (see Figures 5.3 and 5.4).

Screen printing is best approached at Key Stage 2. In order to print a design it is necessary to stretch a fine mesh material over a wooden frame. Allow for a margin around the picture space, about 10 cm, and make sure that the frame is smooth and rigid and that it is lying flat. The thickness of the material will govern the finesse of the design which is ultimately printed. Mesh can be stretched across the screen and secured by hand using staples. Cut the fabric 5 cm larger than the screen and if using silk or nylon dampen it first. The design can then be printed onto card, paper, or fabric and different inks can be used for specific purposes.

Oil based and water soluble inks are both available for printing onto card or paper. The inks that are specially manufactured for the purpose of printing onto fabric consist of pigment that is bound in a water soluble emulsion plus a fixative. Some inks can be purchased ready mixed, others come with the separate binder. The ink is drawn across the screen with a tool called a squeegee that squeezes and pushes the ink through the mesh. The blade is usually made of rubber or plastic and varies in sharpness and flexibility.

Figure 5.3   Print based on a leaf by Hannah

Figure 5.4   Flower print by Lauretta

Working with fabrics and textiles enables children to produce collage work utilising a wide range of materials, ranging from hessian, velvets, felt, furry fabrics and interesting yarns. The feel and use of these materials, and the cutting, sticking, and ensuing sewing skills that support their use, form an important part of primary art. The process of cutting, sewing or sticking pieces of fabric to make dolls, puppets, soft sculptures, various toys, masks or appliqué designs is worthy of its place in the arts programme. Encourage children to select colours carefully, toning and matching threads and textures. Material scraps, such as patterned curtains, dress fabrics, lace, carpeting, braid, ribbon and tape, are very useful. Calico is inexpensive and like white cotton sheeting will dye easily.

Children produce wall hangings, printed and embroidered panels, dresses for puppets, simple costumes, and collage work based on a wide range of themes. Shapes can be applied by using glue or pin, tacked and then sewn. Infant children are capable, under supervision, of creating large fabric appliqué murals. Net, superimposed over a design, will give the effect of haze, or of being under the sea or on a distant planet. Colours can

Figure 5.5 Soft sculpture prototype of a turtle with a woven shell designed and constructed by student teachers

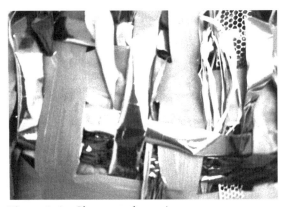

Figure 5.6 Close-up of weaving pattern

be incorporated through the use of fabric paints, crayons, or tie-and-dye techniques. A variety of patterns can be achieved using elastic bands or string on folded, pleated, or gathered fabric which is immersed in cold-water dyes. The soft sculpture of a turtle, designed at Key Stage 2 level, incorporates weaving patterns and textures for the shell. The prototype, illustrated in Figures 5.5 and 5.6 designed and made by student teachers, suggests the possibilities of this method.

Collage is the process of sticking items to a surface to create a picture or design. It combines a variety of materials, colours and textures. If large protruding items are used, then the result is a three-dimensional relief. The adhesive chosen will depend on the type and weight of the materials being stuck together. Always be sure of the safety of glue when working with children. Glue spreaders, brushes or card can be used.

Every material imposes its own discipline, and through its uses children can experiment and learn about its properties. This is particularly pertinent when getting to know about clay through handling it, shaping it, and transforming it from a mass into an organised shape. Encourage exploratory behaviour and foster a positive attitude towards the medium, so that from the initial stages of small hands grasping a lump, children can learn to express ideas that emerge in three-dimensional form. This will occur through the manipulation and problem-solving stages, making decisions about how to shape and form the clay, so that a clay model or vessel emerges. Simply pinching and modelling with the fingers can lead to interesting results and is a viable way of becoming familiar with the texture and properties of clay. Dough is useful for children in the nursery and Reception class. Air-drying clay can be given increased durability through the application of a special hardener. The techniques for bendy materials involve pulling, squeezing, shaping, flattening, coiling, rolling and applying. Artifacts produced range from thumb pots, tiles, coil pots, slab pots, plaques and relief panels.

Construction sculpture is achieved through abstract or representational model-making and construction in the form of 'junk sculpture'. Techniques will include cutting, gluing, fitting and fixing shapes together, joining pieces of wood, card, or other forms of junk. Suitable materials are endless, but include card, balsa wood, soap, soft wood, cane, wooden off-cuts, wire, plastic, *objets trouvée* such as bark, driftwood, bone and shells.

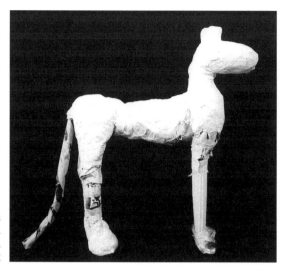

Figure 5.7   Three-dimensional construction using card, wire and plaster-impregnated bandage (mod-rock). Prototype animal model by a student teacher of ongoing work

Mod-rock, as previously mentioned, is a plaster-impregnated fabric bandage sold as strips. An armature of wire netting, wire shapes, wooden structure, or even a balloon forms the base which is covered with dampened newspaper. The mod-rock is then cut to working lengths, immersed in lukewarm water for about three seconds, squeezed gently, and layered onto the basic shape. The surface can be textured while wet and completed models can be painted when dry. This is an ideal material for background features, relief models, masks, landscapes or architectural models. Figure 5.7 shows the construction stage of a prototype animal figure designed and made by a student teacher, the stability of which is dependent upon corrugated card.

Mixed media applies to the combining of one process with another as in the making of costumes, puppetry and masks, but in murals, pictures, sculptures and other imaginative presentations. Stabiles can be constructed from cardboard boxes, bases (made from half a potato, lumps of clay or dough), into which sculptural shapes are formulated using sticks, wire, twigs, mod-rock and other appropriate materials. In contrast, movements of the mobile bring visual interest to the environment. Digital media has a number of possibilities and can be used graphically to illustrate other work in the curriculum or bought as packages that focus on aspects of art. Virtual gallery visits are made possible through the use of the computer and access to web sites.

A basic stock of white drawing paper and coloured sugar paper suitable for individual work, group collages and classroom displays is essential. Water-colour paper has a rough surface, although lightweight cartridge paper is also suitable. Newsprint is inexpensive and is ideal for experimental and practice work, and for papier mâché. The sugar paper comes in assorted colours as does the poster paper rolls. These are generally suitable for drawing, crayon, pastel and collage, including printing. A small stock of special papers, which are a little more expensive, given extra choice according to need and use. Vivid colours, fluorescent colours, tissue paper, crêpe paper, metallic paper, cellophane, gloss surface paper and poster papers all add variety, choice and interest to the art programme. Card and board is expensive so needs to be used with discrimination.

Corrugated cardboard rolls are ideal as backdrops for displaying work, for screens and for sets for drama and dance activities. Some boards are special for scraper work – these may have coloured backing or foil. Wood can be purchased as balsa wood packs, peg kits, craft sticks, match sticks, and as crafted packs. Adhesives that are safe for children are available and include general-purpose adhesives that provide extremely strong adhesion between porous surfaces.

THE PIVOTAL ROLE OF VISUAL ART IN RELATION TO DANCE, DRAMA AND MUSIC

The visual statements that children make in fine art, by means of a wide range of materials and media forms, shows how their management and skilful development is applied to problem-solving situations in much the same manner as in the performance arts. Fine art, produced from understanding the elemental basis of art, focuses on ideas conveyed and contained within the visual image. Spatial arrangement links with choreographic understanding in dance and performance groupings and directional uses of space in drama. The close relationship between visual art and music, in terms of rhythm, pattern, dynamic and emotional content was considered in the previous chapter. Pictorial art and portraiture is representative of the human condition and contains a sense of drama. It provides understanding of people, events and places captured on a particular timescale that allows interpretation. The performing arts bring a living dimension to visual art.

The functional aspects of visual art, craft and design provide a link with dance and drama when children utilise design and construction skills when they make puppets or masks – art objects in their own right that take on greater significance when they are of use. Of equal importance is the collective making of special environments within the classroom, perhaps a corner or central area, encouraging a wide range of learning activities, including drama role-play. Figure 5.8 shows the pivotal role of art in relation to music, dance and drama.

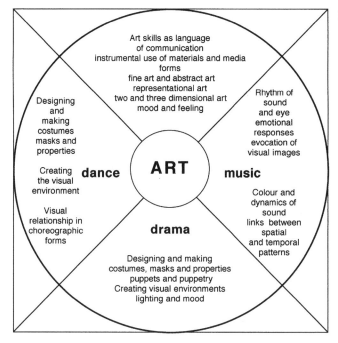

Figure 5.8   The pivotal role of art

VISUAL LITERACY AND THE RESPONSE TO ART

The National Curriculum programmes of study in art, craft and design provide a framework in which the child and the teacher operates. Pedagogical skills are related to the wider understanding of the nature of artistic experience and its meaning and purpose within the context of the primary school. Starting points will emerge, initially, from the sensitive awareness or 'feelings' as experienced by the child acting as a motivator. Visual sensitivity occurs as the teacher provides the opportunity for numerous ways of seeing and ways of expressing what is seen. This is a powerful and vibrant interrelationship upon which all art is based and is brought into play through both investigating and making.

Heightening the child's awareness to visual form will focus on perceptions of colour, line, shape, volume and texture. Ideas will spring from the immediate source of inspiration, and from observing and experiencing the disciplines or techniques the child will acquire the tools of expression. In this way, ideas and impressions are personalised within a particular form and genre and serve to demonstrate the unique response of each individual as they explore and evaluate their own ideas. Confidence in the art-making process is required in order to have successful and valued outcomes. The presentation of work, whether in the individual child's portfolio or as part of an exhibition, reflects both the value of the process and the work produced. It allows children to celebrate their own achievements and respond creatively to each other's work.

Visual appreciation is based on children interpreting what they view as they make and view art. This final process, which leads to critical discussion, is also a form of creative engagement based on reading or understanding the artifact. Visual literacy – the careful training of the eye to look and see and respond – forms the basis of the understanding, whether in terms of observational skills that will kindle creative thought and action as the instigating process, or as a critical power in responding to the finished work. Children, with help from each other and their teacher, discuss the content of a painting and the terminology they use is based on the elements of art as presented in Figure 5.9. As children build up their powers of discussion, they incorporate a vocabulary that has meaning for them from their own creative participation as well as in critical discussion. The metalanguage of art is based on the interpretation and construction of art objects, and is linked to the children's visual perception of specific works of art. Visually perceptive teachers encourage the children to be visually discernible by thoughtfully considering the content and composition of artifacts. Developing visual literacy means educating children to apply their looking in a meaningful way.

RECEIVED WORKS OF ART AND CHILDREN'S CREATIVITY

There are important links between how children perceive a received work of art and how they develop their own creativity of paintings, architecture and sculpture. There are a number of teaching strategies based on a received work. Artifacts are used to enhance the children's understanding of the use of materials and processes, or even working in the style of an artist. This is a practice that requires sensitive understanding to avoid copying or stereotyping. Children's own creativity is helped when learning to use and interpret

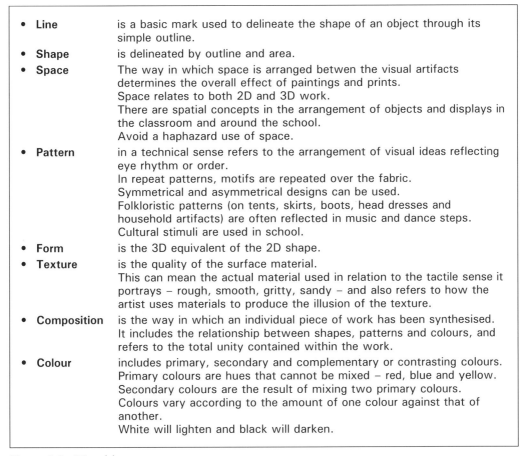

• **Line**	is a basic mark used to delineate the shape of an object through its simple outline.
• **Shape**	is delineated by outline and area.
• **Space**	The way in which space is arranged betwen the visual artifacts determines the overall effect of paintings and prints. Space relates to both 2D and 3D work. There are spatial concepts in the arrangement of objects and displays in the classroom and around the school. Avoid a haphazard use of space.
• **Pattern**	in a technical sense refers to the arrangement of visual ideas reflecting eye rhythm or order. In repeat patterns, motifs are repeated over the fabric. Symmetrical and asymmetrical designs can be used. Folkloristic patterns (on tents, skirts, boots, head dresses and household artifacts) are often reflected in music and dance steps. Cultural stimuli are used in school.
• **Form**	is the 3D equivalent of the 2D shape.
• **Texture**	is the quality of the surface material. This can mean the actual material used in relation to the tactile sense it portrays – rough, smooth, gritty, sandy – and also refers to how the artist uses materials to produce the illusion of the texture.
• **Composition**	is the way in which an individual piece of work has been synthesised. It includes the relationship between shapes, patterns and colours, and refers to the total unity contained within the work.
• **Colour**	includes primary, secondary and complementary or contrasting colours. Primary colours are hues that cannot be mixed – red, blue and yellow. Secondary colours are the result of mixing two primary colours. Colours vary according to the amount of one colour against that of another. White will lighten and black will darken.

Figure 5.9   Visual language

familiar subject matter, or when they are learning how to express ideas and feelings. Making a copy or pastiche has limited creative value but may help critical understanding of style or materials or the rules of composition, depending upon the astuteness of the teacher. References to received works can be used as a means of extending the children's knowledge of the technical and aesthetic aspects of the use of colour, pattern and texture, line and tone, shape, form and space of art works. Methods of critical appraisal include discussing the artist's work, comparing the artist's work and writing about the artist's work. Children need to learn about the artist's life and work, how the work was made and its meaning, as well as the social and cultural context of works. Museum and gallery education officers are important agents in developing work in critical studies.

A way of building up professional confidence is to understand that critical understanding of art should incorporate the critical understanding and ongoing evaluative processes that are inherent within the art of teaching. Self-questioning about intention and output, process and problem-solving stages have direct application to works of art, since there is a relationship between the act of synthesis and the act of analysis. This applies to all the arts and requires an intellectual or academic understanding of how the technical aspects of an art form facilitate creative expression and how, through the artifact, this is communicated. It draws a response which relates to the appreciation and interpretation of the artifact. While common, shared experiences exist, the worth of individual responses and reasons for them must be valued. This means that having an opinion and coming to a judgement are skills that can be taught, but not by prescription and not necessarily in the expectation of acquiring consensus. Understanding about formulating criteria for judgement, whether in terms of what to look for in the received work or in the child's own artifact, is fundamental to meaningful teaching.

CREATING THE VISUAL ENVIRONMENT

Two- and three-dimensional work can be effectively displayed in the classroom, either as separate pieces of work individually mounted or as composite efforts, as for example when groups of children have created a mural. Displays of interestingly shaped or colourful materials that appeal both to the eye and the touch can stimulate work of both an artistic and a scientific nature, and the classroom, corridors and other areas in the school should be transformed into a gallery, showing children's work and that of professional artists. It is important that discrimination and taste is applied so that background colours are subdued and do not detract from the subjects being displayed, and that there is a clear sense of focus. Cluttered lines and over-fussy detail detracts from the art work and creates an unsettling environment.

Objects that excite and stimulate the children can be put out on display so it is important to build a good resource for these means and a collection of the following type and range of materials would be appropriate:

- historical artifacts
- children's toys
- items of clothing
- dolls and dolls' clothing
- machine parts
- natural objects such as rocks, stones, fossils, feathers, twigs, tree bark, roots, dried flowers, dried herbs, leaves and seed boxes
- sea objects such as shells, coral, sand, crab cases, starfish, sea urchins, seaweed, lobster pots, model boats, ship in a bottle, fish nets, driftwood and cork floats
- items from the home such as kitchen utensils, cooking pots, jugs, baskets, bowls, cutlery, wooden trays, old clocks, parts of machines, cogs, wheels, nuts, bolts, screws, tools, scrap metal, pottery, bottles, garden implements and plant pots
- building materials, such as bricks and blocks
- musical instruments
- artifacts from different cultures including rugs, blankets, hats, pictures, artifacts in metal, wood and pots
- prints, paintings, additional photographs and slides.

Displays may be mounted by the teacher using materials that s/he has provided and augmented by items brought to school by the children, or they may be largely composed of the children's own work. Items should be accessible to the children at all times. Careful mounting and arrangement of items is important and should be approached sensitively. Choose background colours and drapes that are appropriate for the nature of the work to be displayed. For example, if the theme is linked with autumn, the main colours used should be brown, gold and russet shades with a subdued background that will reflect the mood created by theses hues. If the theme is machines, background colours such as dark, mid and light grey, with metallic tinges of blue would be more appropriate. Always put backing paper or frieze paper up first, choose a border, and sketch out an outline of your intended display so that the whole project follows a particular design. This will be arrived at with consultation with the children. You will also need to cut out large letters for a title or use a computer print-out. Be sensitive in how you use labelling. It may or may not be necessary depending on the purpose of the display. If it is informative then written information will be part of it, but if the main intention is to excite the visual curiosity then words will detract from the artistry, and so would be inappropriate and undesirable. It would be preferable to produce exhibition notes or notices. A display is there to promote interest and to catch the attention of the onlooker. It should draw the child in, stimulating him/her to think and to be motivated into other learning experiences, whether through the use of language or other artistic modes – movement, music, drama – or through the use of paint, clay or other tangible forms of media. It may also promote an interest in the work of other artists and crafts persons.

VISION AS A MAJOR MODE OF LEARNING

Vision in the newborn child is rudimentary, with sensitive responses to light and darkness. Life involves visual interaction with the environment, but early experiences are often holistic since art represents visually that which is also experienced through other sensations. This develops into the representation of feelings and attitudes as informed by the visual world and through dance and music, or words. Visual images appear as the imagination is stimulated, and children's experiences are heightened when they are asked to imagine things, as teachers provide descriptive information and encourage sensory responses. The representation of the images may well have a point of reference with what has been seen elsewhere. The natural and made environment are source springs for art work, as are examples of other art forms, whether historical or contemporary. Visual sense is a powerful tool for learning and knowledge acquisition. As early as the age of two years, children begin to understand how to use art symbolically, and the power of graphic representation grows stronger with the progress through school. Linked with visual perception is language – the use of appropriate terminology that informs all stages of the art process. Figure 5.9 is a map of basic terms, comprising a vocabulary of visual understanding.

Food, as a project in art, is an appropriate theme at any level of the primary school and can be integrated with other areas of the curriculum. It can be approached in numerous ways:

- investigating through observational drawing in pastel of edible fruits and vegetables – including colour, texture, shape, size and cross-sections
- evidence from collecting photographs, accounts and other graphic representations of fruit put together either as a collage with Reception and Key Stage 1 classes, or in the sketchbooks of older children

- creating artifacts – two-dimensional paintings and collages based on arrangements of fruit, vegetables or cooked food such as bread or three-dimensional models of either giant fruit, a historical banquet or Victorian picnic
- resources of received works depicting how artists have portrayed food.

The systematic development of skills, knowledge and understanding will be specific to visual art so will necessarily include a number of experiences of materials and media, taught in a manner that will achieve high standards including constructive criticism and high expectations.

Aesthetic judgement and artistic evaluation of art works is part of this process and as applied within educational contexts includes the area of assessment, recording and reporting of pupils' progress in and through art. The formulation of viable assessment criteria is vital, so the use and application of language as applied to artistic engagement is of paramount importance. This final stage of the practice of teaching art follows the same model as presented for drama, dance and music, and includes teacher evaluation based on intention, outcome and standard of work produced. Assessment of visual art is applied sensitively and positively.

Educational judgements are based on set criteria and relate to how children conducted themselves in the lesson and the standard of art produced. Observing children, and intervening with help and advice, will ensure successful engagement in their work and show how independence and confidence developed through concentration and self-discipline. Were the children thinking about what they were doing? Did they make efforts to develop their skills, of say two-dimensional work, in order to make artistic judgements in terms of their mark-making? Judgements have to be made about technical aspects of line, form, shape and colour in respect of where these marks were placed on the paper and what meaningful relationship there was between them. The ongoing decision-making reflects the understanding of the child's relationship between the materials used, how they were used and the art-making process. These are important factors in understanding the nature of creativity in visual art. The teacher's role is to help sharpen individual perception and enable children to crystallise ideas within their visual symbol statements.

The method of observation, interaction, clarity of aims and objectives as suggested necessitate an ongoing assessment process. The kind of questions, the manner of intervention, and the nature of the discussion all provide the means of extending the quality of both teaching and learning. Children's progress in visual art can be recorded at intervals as required by the school, based on observational notes relating to work undertaken within each project, and consolidated each term, details of which are considered in Chapter 7 ('Professional Growth').

CHAPTER 6

The Interrelated Curriculum Mode

The requirements of the National Curriculum 2000, although subject based, can be interpreted and taught in a variety of ways, implementing traditional and innovative approaches. Dance, drama, music and visual art, in addition to possessing a unique role as part of the creative and aesthetic area of the curriculum, also possess central and pivotal roles in drawing together other subject areas in the form of integration and interdisciplinary experiences of the primary school. In this way, the arts are both conceived and organised as an integral and central part of every school day. This chapter illustrates how, when primary school children formulate their responses in the performing and visual arts through the use of different forms of expression (sound, movement, voice and art materials), they are also empowered to understand other types of learning within the primary school curriculum. This occurs because diversity and richness are provided by using a number of media forms that address contrasting modes of perception.

THE INTERRELATIONSHIP OF THE ARTS WITHIN THE CURRICULUM

The experiences that children acquire through artistic creativity, as outlined in the previous chapters, is based on a secure understanding of movement, voice, instrumental sounds, and by using a variety of visual art forms. These experiences nurture the imagination and provide skills that can be effectively used as a means of enhancing understanding of other discipline areas. Creative work grows out of each individual arts discipline and its combination with another, and it has been shown how processes take place and artifacts emerge that are rooted in the nature of the arts themselves. They can be of a pure or abstract nature whether musical compositions born out of rhythmical studies, or dance sequences exclusively drawn from dance ideas. Over many generations, artists have absorbed other subject matter into their work, encapsulating and communicating evidence of the world in which they live and choose to comment upon.

In the same manner that the composer, choreographer or painter researches the subject matter of his/her artistic project, so too the information and knowledge that children acquire in their studies of other subject areas of curriculum (as contained within the programmes of study in the National Curriculum) can become the illustrative content of their dances, musical compositions, paintings, sculptures or dramatisations. In so doing, not only can mutual benefit be obtained through sectoral definition and overlap, but children's learning takes on an holistic dimension that brings unity and order to their lives. It also extends children's creative insights by combining ideas or encouraging them to interpret information in new ways. Learning in this manner is multifaceted because it draws upon and develops the exciting interrelationships of the various forms of children's innate intelligence by awakening linguistic, mathematical, spatial, kinaesthetic and musical modes. This permits individual children to conceptualise and understand by using their strength areas to compensate or overcome weaknesses in other areas. It also has the impact of motivating children, sustaining their interest and improving their self-esteem. It provides in-depth study and develops all-round skills.

ASSIMILATING KNOWLEDGE THROUGH THE ARTS

Children learn to conceptualise through several different symbol systems, each of which is a vehicle for thinking and acquiring knowledge. The curriculum is constructed to accommodate diverse ways of acquiring knowledge and understanding through such symbol systems as language (verbal and written), logico-deductive systems of mathematics and science, as well as the visual, aural and kinaesthetic aspects of the arts. Utilising the arts as ways of meaning and understanding emphasises the organic process of learning in which intellectual and motor components of experience are correlated and processed into artifacts. Conceptual understanding in one form of knowledge can be transposed into another form through the process of assimilation. One form does not replicate another, neither is it a substitute for it – its fitness for purpose is based on the meaning which it purports to contain and convey. In terms of the arts, the meaning is based on the interpretation of ideas and feelings, so that for example, the geographical understanding of a particular type of landform or weather systems can be processed and presented as a landscape study in visual art.

The traditional subject base of the National Curriculum is not mutually exclusive but part of a wider epistemological framework that recognises a collection of mutually supportive knowledge areas, including the philosophical, empirical, sociological, historical, religious, mathematical, moral and aesthetic networks. The understanding of one area of knowledge enhances another, so that when children learn about scientific aspects of movement, sound or colour, composition and properties of materials, they are better informed as artists. Equally their accomplishments in the arts can provide a headway into experiencing and understanding other subjects. Children can use the arts to conceptualise about other knowledge areas, when they select scientific, technological, historical, mathematical, religious or geographical themes to be the main focus or illustrative content of their creative work. Their understanding of the subject matter comes through, and is expressed by, the process of the arts and the planning, teaching and learning is based on the teaching integrated arts exemplar, with an added proviso that examines the appropriateness of the subject matter to lend itself to artistic expression. What aspect of the topic of study – English, mathematics, science, design technology, history, geography, religious education – can be understood through, or provide the stimulus for, dance, drama, music or visual art?

APPLYING AN EXEMPLAR MODEL

Figure 6.1 illustrates a framework for a mutually supportive curriculum that permits children to learn aspects of science, humanities, technology and mathematics through the arts. It is based on the main areas of learning as required by the National Curriculum and is designed to encourage creative thought and action by utilising a variety of learning skills in a developmental and progressive manner. The method of approach, from planning, execution and evaluation of teaching, follows the same principles as expounded in the exemplar model, Seascape (see Chapter 1), but substituting the main theme of the sea by one taken from a programme of study from a specific curriculum area. The methodology is as follows:

- select the curriculum area which is to be interrelated with the arts
- identify the main area of learning within it that can stimulate or inform the arts
- analyse the main area of learning in terms of artistic interpretation in drama, dance, music and visual art
- identify how the arts can be integrated.

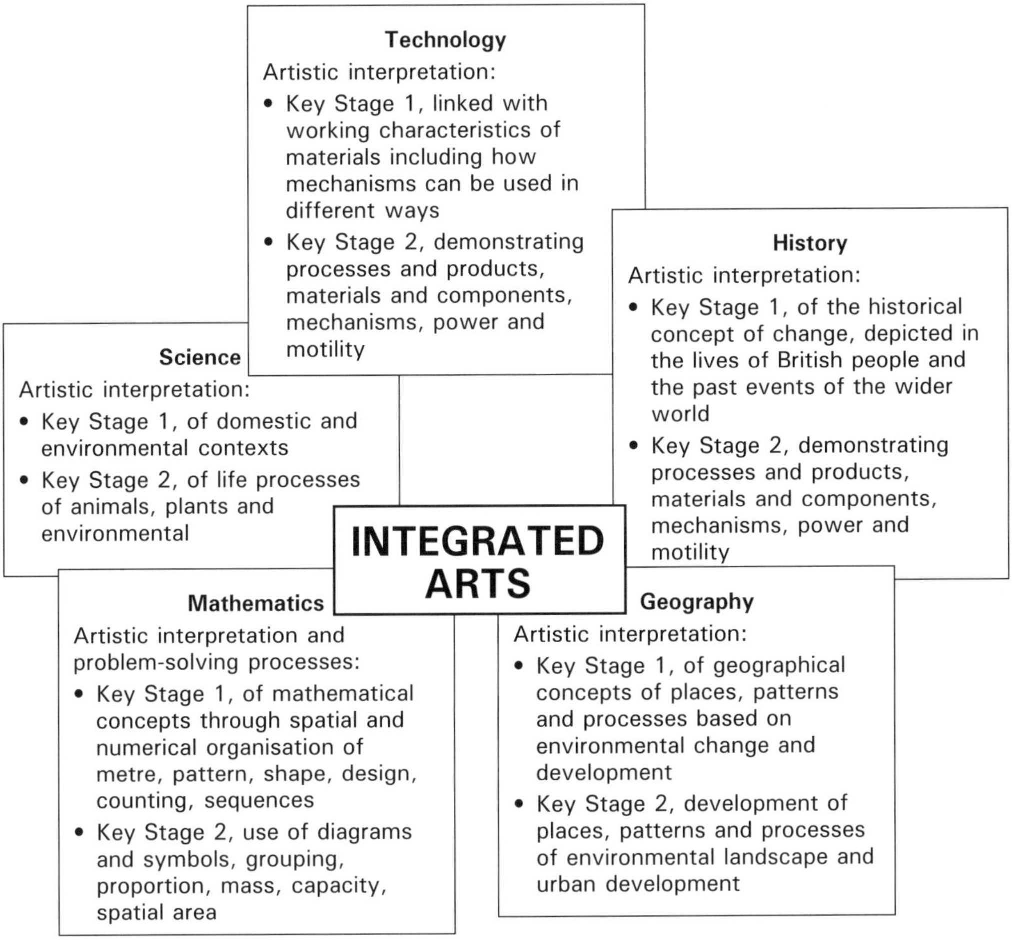

Technology
Artistic interpretation:
- Key Stage 1, linked with working characteristics of materials including how mechanisms can be used in different ways
- Key Stage 2, demonstrating processes and products, materials and components, mechanisms, power and motility

History
Artistic interpretation:
- Key Stage 1, of the historical concept of change, depicted in the lives of British people and the past events of the wider world
- Key Stage 2, demonstrating processes and products, materials and components, mechanisms, power and motility

Science
Artistic interpretation:
- Key Stage 1, of domestic and environmental contexts
- Key Stage 2, of life processes of animals, plants and environmental

INTEGRATED ARTS

Mathematics
Artistic interpretation and problem-solving processes:
- Key Stage 1, of mathematical concepts through spatial and numerical organisation of metre, pattern, shape, design, counting, sequences
- Key Stage 2, use of diagrams and symbols, grouping, proportion, mass, capacity, spatial area

Geography
Artistic interpretation:
- Key Stage 1, of geographical concepts of places, patterns and processes based on environmental change and development
- Key Stage 2, development of places, patterns and processes of environmental landscape and urban development

Figure 6.1   An interrelated curriculum through integrated arts

The following section includes a number of working exemplars in the integrated arts using illustrative content from other modes of study and experiences contained within the National Curriculum. Comment on teaching and learning approaches demonstrate the application of systematic planning, recording and reporting of assimilation experiences with children at Reception to Key Stages 1 and 2. Each curriculum area is reviewed polemically in respect of: the artistic interpretation and expression of one specific element of study as forming the illustrative content of drama, dance, music or art within an integrated arts mode; how the learning parameters of a specific curriculum area can stimulate or inform artistic understanding. Implementing the integrated arts within the interrelated curriculum mode draws upon the six key skills which are embedded in the National Curriculum – communication, application of number, information technology, working with others, improving own learning and performance, and problem solving. Education in and through the arts challenges the way both children and teachers understand about *how* they think as well as knowing *what* to think about. Thinking skills that are drawn upon in the interrelated curriculum mode include information-processing skills, reasoning skills, enquiry skills, creative thinking skills and evaluative skills.

WORKING EXEMPLARS OF THE INTERRELATED CURRICULUM MODE

English

Previous chapters have illustrated how the knowledge, skills and understanding of English is important in teaching and learning dance, music and the visual arts. Chapter 2 ('The Drama Mode') focused on the language and literary skills implicit in this art form. Approaches towards speaking and listening, and the use of group discussion as part of the process of learning the arts, complements the additional skills of reading and writing linked to discussion and written critical responses. The use of English prose and poetry, fiction and non-fiction are the raw materials upon which practical interpretations and implementations are based. There are numerous popular stories and written sources from children's books which can be readily used for drama, dance, music and visual art – mythology, fairy and folk-tales, legends and ballads, narrative, lyrical and action poems.

Key Stage 1

The following suggestions for an integrated arts project are based on the popular narrative poem, *We're Going on a Bear Hunt*. The ideas are based on a teaching experience that took place in Western Australia when the stimulus was an environmental orienteering project hunting down a toy bear hidden in the bushland. The narrative, with solo voice and responsorial for chorus, provides the structural framework around which the main dramatic and dance action takes place. Musical sound effects with specific sound pictures can also be used in conjunction with a mural and environment constructed as part of art. The dance and drama are presented to children as a series of sectional workshops lasting around 15–20 minutes leading to a movement enactment of the whole story, with groups of children joining in throughout the session. Each section is either presented each day or over a period of weeks and constitutes part of the children's movement repertoire. The sections commence with a warm-up that provides contrasting movements which incorporate whole body and specific body actions related to the theme, introducing new ideas and recapitulating on what went before. Workshops include actions for specific body parts and whole body actions and should stimulate and encourage the child's personal artistic growth as well as the physical, mental, social and emotional aspects. In terms of music, the use of instruments to create mood music reflecting each or selected parts of the story can be presented as compositional pieces. These can be prerecorded if used as accompaniment to dance. The main events of the story, presented as a scenario with six scenes, start with the description of a beautiful day in the meadow and the commencement of the bear hunt, progressing to the adventures of crossing the river, negotiating the thick mud, traversing the dark forest, entering the cave, and culminating in the confrontation with the bears and the hasty retreat back home to the safety of a warm, snug bed.

We're Going on a Bear Hunt

The main learning content will be organised around the following scenes:

- A Beautiful Day
- A Deep Cold River
- Thick Oozy Mud
- A Big Dark Forest
- A Narrow Gloomy Cave
- The Retreat

Scene 1 – A Beautiful Day

This is a creation in dance and drama of the meadow of long wavy grass. Children use fingers, hands, arms and legs as grass growing and waving. Meadow flowers, wild flowers and dandelions are portrayed through the shape of hands. The musical picture is of a beautiful day – melodic line of sunshine, breeze and long grass growing (crescendo). Gentle rhythm represents frolicking bears and silence when the bears have hidden. In visual art create a classroom mural of a beautiful day. Use sponge printing for background colours of the landscape, brush strokes for the long grass growing, and collage for the bears.

Scene 2 – A Deep Cold River

Moving like the river is portrayed by reaching and stretching slowly in circular directions following the leader suggesting the long tail of the river. Cross the river. Create a musical picture of the river by making water sounds with xylophone, maracas and voice. In visual art delineate the flowing river on the mural with appliqué of blue, grey, white and green materials fixed in to form a bas-relief.

Scene 3 – Thick Oozy Mud

Dance and drama recap meadow movements which become slower and gradually get heavier as if travelling through mud. Make movements that are heavy and ponderous – slowly rolling, creeping and crawling, pulling out hands, knees, elbows and head. Musically, depict slow, heavy, ponderous sounds with percussion instruments to accompany the voice. In visual art study earth colours from rich brown through to creamy clay colours. Experiment with texture using powder paint and monoprints which continue the bas-relief.

Scene 4 – A Big Dark Forest

Dance and drama recap on earlier experiences then make a forest of bodies. Children follow their partner through the forest. The bears are in the forest. In music use climbing up the scale to suggest growth, with stops and starts reflecting the rhythm. Use a variety of instruments introduced in succession to suggest many trees growing. Underpin this with a frolicking rhythm of the bears. In art use cylindrical shapes to represent trees, made either individually or in small groups and attach them to a mural.

Scene 5 – A Narrow Gloomy Cave

Dance and drama recap on earlier activities – through the meadow, through the river, through the mud and through the forest. Children make individual shapes – rounded and curled with weight on different parts of the body. Small groups of children appear rounded and cave-like, making the shapes of boulders and stones, stalagmites and stalactites. They form a circle and move closer together to make the circle become a cave shape. Children take turns to explore the cave. Musically, the children will create the sound picture to inspire the action and the environment, making echo sounds, eerie sounds and using voice and instruments to maximum effect. Create at first a romantic depiction of the cave, then increase the tempo, suggesting expectation and excitement, and end with a dramatic crescendo as the climax when the bear is discovered. Visual art work will complete the mural with the creation of the cave, by extending the bas-relief using irregular rock shapes, depicting the angularity and sparkle of crystals, and smooth columns of stalagmites. The hanging stalactites can be constructed as a mobile.

Scene 6 – The Retreat

The final session brings the other five scenes together in reverse order, so dance, drama and music will depict a snowy day with movements and sounds that whirl, swirl, rise and fall. Suggest to the children that the snow whirls around in the wind and gently settles down on the floor like a huge blanket. Encourage them to use all the space and imagine the blanket to be the blanket in bed. Dance out the last section which is the retreat, but then *you* forgot to shut the door – quickly go back downstairs and shut the door, return to bed and hide. Musically, suggest the cosiness of bed with the gentle ticking of a clock.

Key Stage 2

At Key Stage 2 children utilise their knowledge, skills and understanding of speaking, listening, reading and writing within the context of an integrated arts programme, through discussion of creative arts processes, critical responses, and through the use of literary stimuli, whether poetry, story or dramatic forms. The following scenario for a court masque uses John Milton's *Comus* as the stimulus. Milton wrote *Comus* before becoming engaged in the important affairs of the state during the Commonwealth period. It was first performed in 1634 at Ludlow by members of the Earl of Bridgewater's family, for whom the work was composed, but the scenario as presented here is based on workshops that took place at Clifton Hall, Nottinghamshire, and Bolsover Castle, Derbyshire. *Comus* is both mythological and allegorical in content and follows a simple but mystical narrative. The words and music still exist but little is known of the exact nature of the dancing. *Comus* depicts virtue in the form of Alice, the Earl's daughter, who is lost in a forest and threatened by a magician and his rout of primordial followers. Alice is protected by the Attendant Spirit, who upon the successful completion of his task ascends to heaven amidst proclamations of morality and virtue. Interpretations of the text suggest that the dances performed were familiar to both performers and spectators, since they included examples of both court and country dances, rather than containing specially choreographed works. Introduce the children to the experience by saying what the intentions are and their role, with a careful explanation of the relevant historical background to the activities. Commence with a grand procession to the accompaniment of baroque music, thereby establishing a style of deportment and imagining the style of period costume. If possible, use dressing-up clothes. Present the narrative of the masque so that the children can visualise and work through the drama, determining the roles, positions and actions of the players. After compiling the masque, practise it all through a number of times finishing with the performance of the country dance, *Sellinger's Round*, by all the company. Figures 6.2 and 6.3 are sketches based on drama workshops with children in historical settings.

Comus – A masque for children

Scene 1 – Ludlow Castle

The children are gathered in the Great Chamber of Ludlow Castle. The Earl of Bridgewater and his family, including his daughter Alice, will present the masque.

> CHORUS   Meanwhile welcome Joy and Feast,
> Midnight shout, and revelry,
> Tipsie dance, and Jollity[1]

Scene 2 – A Mysterious Forest

Children make the shape of the forest and enact its changing mood.

> VOICE 1   Who in their nightly watchful Sphears,
> Lead in swift round the Months and Years.
> VOICE 2   The Sounds, and Seas with all their finny drove
> Now to the Moon in wavering Morrice move,
> VOICE 3   And on the Tawny Sands and Shelves,

Figure 6.2   A sketch of the children's drama workshop – *Comus*

Figure 6.3   A sketch of children's role-play in a heritage environment

1. Milton, J. (1634) *Comus*, The Oxford Book of English Verse (first published 1900).

	Trip the pert Fairies and the dapper Elves;
Voice 4	By dimpled Brook, and Fountain brim,
	The Wood-Nymphs deckt with Daisies trim,
	Their merry wakes and pastimes keep:
All voices	What hath night to do with sleep?

The forest is inhabited by an evil magician, Comus, and his half animal/half human followers who want to capture the children and turn them into half/beasts. Enter Comus and his rout who dance around in a circle. Other children mime the antics of the animals and hide, with Comus, like statues behind the trees. Alice and her younger brother enter the forest.

Scene 3 – *In the Depths of the Mysterious Forest*

They become lost in the forest. They try to return home but the trees enclose them. They lie down to sleep. They are plagued by Comus and his rout, who surround them and dance menacingly round them. Enter the Attendant Spirit who protects the children by turning Comus and the rout into stone statues. The Attendant Spirit leads Alice and her brother safely back to Ludlow Castle. Attendant Spirit speaks:

> And not many furlongs thence
> Is your father's residence,
> Where this night are met in state
> Many a friend to gratulate
> His wished presence, and beside.
> All the strains that there abide
> With jigs and rural dance resort

Scene 4 – *The Great Chamber at Ludlow Castle*

All the Company rejoice in a dance *Sellinger's Round*. The creative work in music will include leitmotifs for the characters in the story, composition of mood music for the forest at night, a rhythmical dance for Comus and his rout, and music of joy for the happy ending. The traditional music of *Sellinger's Round* will be used for the dance, either played on recorders or using recorded music.

Creative work in visual art and design will include paintings, pictures or murals of the enchanted forest, a collage of the children acting out the masque either as miniature or life-size models, and the construction of masks for Comus and his followers.

Comus gives children the opportunity to gain confidence within a specific context of the masque, in which they can adapt their speech for a peer audience. Improvising and recording script will facilitate the use of new vocabulary in order to gain and maintain the interest and response by reflecting the beauty of the poetry for the mystical and magical effects, and the use of their own words to convey fear and excitement. It provides opportunity for children to speak audibly and clearly within a formal context, especially as this masque can be adapted and performed in the location of a heritage site. Music, dancing, singing and the performance of masques were popular pastimes in the seventeenth century and followed a tradition extending back to medieval times. Contextual evidence will support the children's own creativity.

The story form

Narrative relates to all areas of the curriculum and lends itself to artistic interpretation by focusing on selected aspects only – some parts to listen to, others to act out, and sections to integrate and use as stimuli for creative interpretation. Mythology is a vast area and it is suggested that teachers select stories that are available for children to read, listen to as music or watch as extracts of ballets. The Appendix (see page 145) includes a range of published materials that can be used.

Maths

Knowledge, skills and understanding of mathematical concepts can be both helped and utilised through the arts. Number, shape, space and measures all come into being either as steps and sequences in dance and music, shape and spatial relationships in dance and art, and measure in terms of judgement of construction materials or choreographic placing. The processes of the arts help to develop flexible approaches to problem solving and encourage children to look for ways of seeking solutions. The discipline of composition, whether in dance or music means that children organise and check their work and, through the precision of language, symbols and vocabulary, communicate their findings. Symbol systems of musical and dance notation, graphics and sounds recorded by a computer are all used. At Key Stage 1, counting relates to music and dance actions, and rhythmical and dynamic content can lead to the understanding of number patterns and sequences.

At Key Stage 2 children's reasoning skills are further developed and used in terms of the ordering, placing, selecting and organisation of artistic elements, whether related to the time and pitch qualities of music, or the timing and pattern qualities of dance, or the rational judgements in determining motif repeats in visual art. Problem solving in mathematics is a form of decision-making that leads to solutions and is a thinking process governed by mathematical factors. Similar processes apply in the arts since the problem-solving process is an inherent skill of creative activity, working through ideas to achieve end results, either choreographically, musically or spatially, by finding different ways of approaching a problem in order to achieve the intended outcome. Children can be taught to break down learning processes into simple stages and work through their ideas to build up greater complexity. Although music and dance have their own conventional notational systems based on symbol systems, it is also possible for children to develop their own methods of recording sound and music by devising their own symbol systems and including digital means as ways of communicating ideas to generate new work or as a record of completed work. In dance, especially, the use of spatial forms can be explored using the grid format as shown in Figure 6.4, which is an adaptation of Froebel's dance forms (Froebel 1909), originally intended to be used with small wooden blocks.

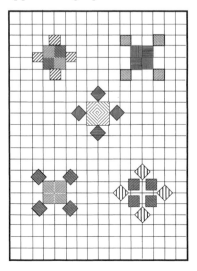

Figure 6.4   Choreographic forms using computer graphics

Using mathematics as a stimulus for the arts can be achieved when using specific ideas and linking them appropriately with either drama, dance, music or art. In the case of drama through the dramatisation of important mathematical discoveries, particularly those that have influenced scientific and technological progress. Approached from an integrative perspective, the topic of architecture and buildings successfully encapsulates a number of mathematical concepts that conjoin with artistic principles. The following framework provides opportunities at either Key Stages 1 and 2, and is based on the analysis of a specific building. Choices can be taken from the locality, nationally or internationally, related to the present or to the past, and can include the principal buildings of towns and villages and cities, or refer to examples around the world (past, present and future).

Architecture and buildings

Observation and analysis of architectural features

Consider the plan as a bird's eye view and approach exterior and interior perspectives. Think about:

- exteriors – north, south, east, west elevations, walls, windows, facade, colonnade, roof and doors, plumbing (pipes and drainage), chimney stacks and chimney pots, brickwork and mortar patterns, balustrade, mouldings, wings, light-wells and sky lights
- interiors – walls, windows, window shutters, doors and porticoes, chimney pieces and fireplaces, skirting boards, sconces that held candles, balustrades, stairs, pillars/columns, capitals and orders of architecture (Doric, Ionic, Corinthian, Composite); pilasters, dome/cupola, arches, classical pediments, ceilings and friezes
- building materials and construction methods – walls of stone, brick, cement, marble, plaster, wood, glass, ceramic tiles, cast iron and wrought iron
- style – mediaeval, Elizabethan, Jacobean, Carolean, Georgian, Victorian, modern, post-modern, futuristic
- uses – for what purpose was the building erected, home or industry, leisure or worship?

Using photographic evidence and standard texts for:

- home use – furniture design and style showing chairs, tables, clocks, musical instruments, beds, baths, dressing tables, screens, nursery furniture, pictures, mirrors, library books, curtains, wallpaper designs. Style and design of kitchen, pantry, larder, cellar
- industrial use – machinery and industrial processes, modern canteen, restaurant, rest facilities
- commercial use – airport, train station, bus station
- place of worship – nave, aisle, alter, chapel, vestry, tower, spire.

Artistic interpretation

Visual analysis of line, colour, form and shape provides valuable information. Analyse line as expressed in diagrams, plans, sketches, features and viewpoints through mark-making. Examine colour in the exterior and interior light and shade, the mixing and matching of hues and tones, and the use of warm and cold colours, rich, pale, opaque. Capture that which is old and antique or new and vibrant. Consider form in the shape and volume, relationships of features, proportion, dimensions, symmetry, asymmetry, spatial relationships of windows, doors, porticoes and chimney pieces, pillars, pilasters, columns and capitals, towers, domes, spires and turrets.

A wide range of materials and media forms can be offered to the children according to their age and experience including drawing, painting, three-dimensional construction for models, sticking, pasting, cutting, sewing, modelling of clay, plaster, or papier mâché. It is plausible that stone, wood, metal, glass, plaster, basket work, ceramics, earthenware, china, and silver are represented through the use of different types of materials and media and the associated techniques. Figure 6.5 is a prototype model of a neo-classical style building.

Interpretation of the theme through the performing arts will be based on the uses and purposes of the building which will provide the stimulus for drama, either using voice, sound pictures, mime or the production or interpretation

Figure 6.5 Prototype three-dimensional model of a neo-classical style building designed and constructed by a student teacher

of play scripts. Cross-links can be made with history if the building is old. In music, sound pictures will be related to the type and nature of the building, the people who use it, reflecting rhythmical patterns of work and leisure and the tonal significance of the period being portrayed. Listening to extracts of recorded music that have specific connections with buildings include Mussorgsky's musical picture of the old castle from *Pictures at an Exhibition*, choral music, Gregorian chants, Beatle's lyrics and dance suites.

Architecture and dance have a special relationship in terms of spatial significance, and in the manner in which body relationships and constructions contain and reflect tension and counter tension, when bridge, arch and dome shapes are expressed in partner and group work. Of equal significance is the delineation of architectural form through space patterns.

Science

Scientific concepts can be endorsed and discovered through accessing the arts in many different ways. At Key Stage 1 themes connected with life processes and living things, the properties of different materials and physical processes all lend themselves to artistic interpretation, whether depicting the sounds of rain drops in musical composition or the metamorphosis of a hungry caterpillar as movement drama, to the production of paintings, models or classroom environments in visual art. The topics chosen will reflect the immediate domestic and local environmental context familiar to young children, ranging from singing games and actions about, for example, nursery clocks, mechanical toys, historical toys, or kitchen implements and the way in which they work. Active engagement helps children to understand mechanical concepts of motility as expressed through robot dances or drama adventures in outer space. Experimental use of instruments leads to the creation of musical interludes depicting seasonal change while their visual art representations of the wonders of nature are important ways of unifying learning experiences.

At Key Stage 2, the science programme offers a wide range of topics that can be used as stimuli and content of children's artistic creativity. The life processes of animals and plants found in the local environment can be expressed through drama (plays, readings, dramatisations, mimes, puppets); dance (growth, habitat, interaction, prey, survival); music (songs, stories, accompaniment, adventure); and visual art, when animals and plants provide the main source for investigation in the sketchbook and then production in two- or three-dimensional forms. Examples of the received works of art inspired by animals and plants of the English countryside abound and studies can be enhanced with contrasting examples that extend beyond the immediate environment.

Active engagement in the arts through viewing, speaking, listening, and performing (both bodily and instrumentally) are living testimonies to the study of the senses. They can complement scientific recognition and comparison of the main external parts of human bodies and those of other animals, and also the senses that enable people and animals to be cognitive of the world around them as required in the science programme of study. Children's own artistic development and output is based on ways in which the mind and the senses harmoniously conjoin, working within the technical and aesthetic realms of drama, dance, music and art. The scientific knowledge, skills and understanding which children acquire as they study aspects of domestic and environmental contexts can be linked with the arts, either as enactment, performance or visual record. Scientific concepts also underpin understanding of the arts themselves, whether the human body, the science of human movement, the relationship of movement to gravity and space, or the science of sound and colour. Figure 6.6, a prototype paper sculpture of a dolphin, shows art work linked to an environmental theme using appropriate techniques for group work at Reception or Key Stage 1.

Figure 6.6   Environmental study of a dolphin. Prototype designed and constructed by a group of student teachers

Design technology

The technological knowledge, skills and understanding that children acquire are highly supportive to their work in the arts, both conceptually and practically. The process of developing ideas, planning and making products has clear parallels with artistic processes. At some stage there can be mutual overlap, in particular where visual art activities are of an applied nature, but the distinctive qualities must also be acknowledged, especially in the area of fine art. Generating ideas, working creatively with different types of materials, discovering the nature and properties of materials and evaluating work as it progresses through solution seeking, are work methods that artists and technologists share. Similarly, the handling and use of tools, the production of plans and prototypes and the discovery of the uses of materials have practical benefits that can support clarity of approach in the arts. The interchange of ideas as children discuss their work is also mutually beneficial.

The mechanical concepts of technology have a direct bearing on the understanding of human movement, especially when considering the way in which movement can be deconstructed to basic elemental components. Repetitive movements of body parts taken in isolation, emphasising the sequential flow of movement and the nature of the joint action, can help children to understand motility of machines and the sources of power and energy. Rotational, axle, reciprocal, rising and falling, advancing and retreating, accelerating and decelerating, repetitive rhythms executed with bound flow qualities allow children to absorb and express technological concepts. Similarly, mimetic actions and songs, sounds and stories relating to the stages of food preparation and the celebration and festive occasions of eating bring about great opportunities for teachers and children.

Appropriate integrated arts themes at Reception and Key Stage 1 based on technological concepts will include such areas as: how things move, machines, robots, food, clothes, musical instruments and the technology of sound and the story of a product. These areas of study will be interpreted and expressed using stories, poems, music, paintings, and sculptures.

The same principles of interrelationship applied at Key Stage 1 also apply for work at Key Stage 2, and the inclusion of the aesthetic aspects of technological design reinforces the work in the arts. Equally, the greater complexity of the techniques and the skills acquired through the use of equipment and tools will improve manual dexterity in visual art work. Children can apply their understanding of the working characteristics of materials learned in technology to art lessons, especially when working on sculptural ideas. Knowledge of how mechanical components work will transfer to dance lessons about machines and processes of manufacture, and work in textiles has a direct bearing on printing, dyeing, soft sculpture and the making of masks and puppets, the making of a puppet theatre and property items used in drama.

Appropriate integrated arts themes emanating from the design technology studies at Key Stage 2 will extend earlier work to incorporate more complex systems, and will include such aspects as: transport, communication systems, electricity and circuits, structures and forces, fairgrounds, product systems, food processes and textiles.

History

There are close links between history and the arts, since each art area has its own historical contexts which children can experience through critical understanding as well as by bringing the past alive by performing extracts from plays, musical pieces and dances. The creative use of the arts can be used as means of investigating the past, whether through dramatic role-play and the discussion of issues, or by developing key points of an art form by encouraging children to respond through contemporary idioms. For example, looking at early musical or dance forms and responding creatively, or by studying Tudor portraiture and producing portraits of other children in the class using different materials and media (avoid copying existing works).

Historical interpretation through the arts is a valuable and viable form of learning in and through the arts, recognising creative potential and avoiding pastiche. The arts enhance children's understanding of past events and how change impacts upon lifestyle. The arts represent the changing world of the past, they document the changing fashions of music, dance, theatre, architecture, furniture, literature, and it is by making references to past styles in their own lives that children comprehend the importance of the arts as chronicles and comments on the passing of time. Visual reference points and active engagement permit children to understand and identify the manner in which the past is represented. The effective use of heritage sites, museums and galleries, as well as ICT based resources that encourage the use of the arts, is of mutual benefit in aiding children to advance their knowledge of history and the arts. Engaging in traditional singing games and dances are relevant and as much part of the life of the present-day child as of the children of yesteryear, and through historical reference can help children to grasp the concept of change and time gone by. Role-play, use of costumes and historical or reproduction artifacts enable children to understand and express the changes of the past, initially through reference to family and local community and then leading to the studies of the more distant past of British and selected world history.

Events surrounding the lives of artists, especially if approached from the perspective of children either as the subject of paintings or as members of the artist's own family, act as a suitable stimulus. The dramatisation of history is part of a long-established tradition in English education, but the incorporation of visual art work and musical representation of scenes and events from the past can be constructed in an integrated way, celebrating historical happenings that are of interest and relevance to young children – perhaps the invention of the steam locomotive, the discovery of new lands, the opening of new bridges or other engineering feats, the migration of people, travelling and settling in new lands or scenes depicting the lives of kings, queens, emperors or saints.

The following short scenario uses the *Gest of Robin Hood* as the stimulus, and is based on life in a medieval manor house at the time of a boy knight, Sir Gervase Clifton (1313–1391) and Lady Margaret Clifton, who lived at Clifton House, some five miles south of Nottingham Castle overlooking the River Trent.

The boy knight

The scene is a local manor, Clifton House in 1327. A medieval banquet is being hosted by Sir Gervase Clifton (1313–1391) the 14-year-old boy knight, and Lady Margaret Clifton, his lady.

Scene 1

This scene opens with a processional dance and slow line dance (farandole).

Scene 2

The travelling players arrive and perform different scenes of the Greenwood based on the *Gest of Robin Hood*, a ballad depicting adventures of Robin Hood which was written around *c*.1323. Include creating the forest through movement, voice sounds and percussion portraying the outlaws in the forest, woodland animals and the Sheriff riding through.

Scene 3
The jesters and acrobats perform, providing entertainment.

Scene 4
This is the celebration of the company, including circle dance, basse dance and ballad.

Integrating visual art with dance, drama and music will be based on the various locations of the ballad depicting castles, manor houses or woodland, inhabitants of the forest, animals and people, scenes from the stories, designs based on animals and trees, including floriate heads and masks. Costume design and the general style of the times in terms of cooking pots, drinking vessels, knives, plates and serving dishes, food items and furniture provide ample scope for two- or three-dimensional work. Large-scale work, including the use of cardboard boxes and painted or printed wall hangings in tapestry style, will provide a small area in the classroom for imaginative play.

At Key Stage 2, the integrated arts are one of the most appropriate ways in which children, through active and creative engagement, can gain knowledge and understanding of the characteristic features of selected periods and societies of the past, since it is through the arts that these societies have themselves conveyed their own ideas, beliefs and attitudes. The use of instrumental sounds, appropriate dialogue and movement can capture and convey the range of social, cultural, ethnic and religious diversity of specific historical scenes related to Britain and other countries of the world. The interpretation and appreciation of received works of art and other historic resources enable children to build their own scenes from history. These can be based on the reality of a constructed classroom environment with the use of properties, or may take place entirely in the realms of the imagination. Historical understanding through enactment and visual representation relates to the effective interpretation of resources and evidence found in numerous locations pertaining to various forms, whether musical scores, dance scores, drama scripts, paintings, pictures, sculptures, poetry, documents such as letters, diaries and monetary accounts, printed information and electronic sources. When children perform traditional dances or music, and learn extracts of plays from the past (especially Shakespearian drama) they are communicating what they know about the arts and history. Historical knowledge as part of heritage education entails visiting museums, galleries and sites which will inspire the teacher to provide interesting and creative learning experiences for the children.

There is a wide choice of materials within the programme of study at Key Stage 2, and primary school teachers are both familiar and knowledgeable about the content which is based on local, national, European and global areas of study – all of which to some greater or lesser degree facilitate interpretation in and through the integrated arts. Topics of study, based on Britain before the Norman Conquest, include the Romans, the Anglo-Saxons and the Vikings showing how British society was affected. A detailed study of the events and individuals of the Tudor period will lead to an understanding of aspects of everyday life as experienced by different sectors of Tudor society, with Shakespeare's life and plays as a reference point. Similarly, the study of the impact of eminent people, events and changes in lifestyle that took place in Victorian Britain will reflect contrasting features of the time, and draw upon the wealth of Victorian art, music and drama available. The topic of Britain since 1930 will focus on the social and technological changes that have influenced society, drawing upon accessible sources of information from magazines, photographs and other media sources.

The study of Ancient Greece will show how the way of life, philosophical and religious beliefs including the scholarship, physical prowess and the architectural ideals of Ancient Greece have influenced the contemporary world. The study of ancient civilisations is selected from Ancient Egypt, Ancient Sumer, the Assyrian Empire, the Indus Valley, the Maya, Benin, or the Aztecs.

Ancient Egypt

The exploration and description through dance, drama, music and visual art will be inspired by ideas and experiences arising from:

- history, mythology, people and landscape including images based on landscape of the country – fertile plain, river delta, desert
- creation of the animals and people from the sun-dried mud of the river Nile (the Vault of the sky formed by the goddess Nut)
- significance of annual flood, fertility of crops
- people living on the land – occupational tasks, worship of gods, belief in life after death and building tombs for the pharaohs (Osiris or Isis was the god of death who rose up from his grave as a symbol of rebirth).

Sources that give clues to the lives of Egyptian people include the tomb paintings, for example, *Work in the Fields* – a painting in the (east wall of) the tomb built for Sennutem at Deir el Medina. The dead man and his wife share in the work: reaping, ploughing, threshing and sifting the corn. Other tomb paintings depict hunting, sailing, fishing, surveying and building. *Banquet – feasting and dancing* shows the tomb of Nakht, Sheikh Abd el-Kurna (Thebes), and depicts feasting on fine foods and luscious fruits. A lady is smelling a lotus flower, the musicians are playing and girls perform lively, acrobatical dances. *Journey of the Sun* in the tomb of Rameses VI (Valley of the Kings) depicts the happiest hours of the dead, when the boat of the sun, the god Ra came down and carried out its night journey bringing light to the underworld. The 'book of Gates' describes the 12 hours and the incidents for each hour. One of the gates was guarded by a fearsome snake which had to let the boat through. Depict scenes from this journey and the battle to pass through the gates or caverns. Apep, the great serpent, was the perpetual enemy who lived in the depths of the Nile and sometimes caused a total eclipse when he swallowed the barge. Gods included on tomb paintings have human form with animal heads – jackal, falcon, scarab (beetle), vulture and viper.

Other sources of ideas for the arts on this theme arise from sculptural form, rebirth, mummified entombed/hours of freedom, warfare and conquest, capture and homage, water, fertile valley and desert, light and darkness, plenty, famine and plague, the pyramid and the sphynx.

Geography

Geographical understanding can be expressed artistically, especially when approached from the concept of the living earth which is constantly undergoing change either from the elements themselves or because of human intervention. The patterns and processes of environmental change and the way in which the world's resources are utilised are ethical as well as scientific issues, and children's understanding of them can be effectively expressed through the arts. The skills that children acquire as part of geographical enquiry empowers them to use their information as resource materials for the arts, recording ideas and expressing a viewpoint through drama, dance, music and art.

A building will be used by people for a particular purpose – a factory, a shop, a market place – with a variety of modes of transport, each of which can be recorded visually by models, dances and songs. Geographical terms can be expressed both literally and metaphorically – hills, valleys, mountains, rivers, rock formations, caves, pinnacles, hollows, rifts, volcanoes and lava flows, flood plains, deltas, sand dunes, rain forests, railway lines and roads. The hall space is transformed into a different environment and by individual, partner and group activities environmental dances are choreographed. The blank sheet is filled with visual ideas: colours, shapes, textures made into murals or environments depicting deserts, rain forests, tundra, or cityscapes. Weather patterns, the water cycle and sources of power can each be effectively interpreted. Work songs and mime dances reflect work patterns of crop growth and harvest throughout the world, contrasting with the mechanical actions and sounds of farm machinery. The following ideas are based on using the theme of weather as an integrated arts project providing many possibilities for visual interpretation and expression through drama, dance and music.

Weather

Children develop each specific art form in order to acquire the means of expression through the relevant techniques of drama, dance, music and art. For example they may use the spatial significance and body awareness in dance along with the melodic line and rhythmical structure of music to conjure up cloud formation leading to thunder and rainfall. They may work on a structure of action and stillness matching with musical crescendo, climax and silence as children create individual sequences. Developing the pattern and form of a weather dance follows the natural sequence of the scientific change of weather conditions. Quality of sound and movement match these changes. Weather can be related to any of the world's climatic zones. The following ideas are related to the tropical storm and suggest the source of creative imagery as related to:

- rainstorm, sunshine and shadow
- reflections in a forest pool
- thunderous rolls, heavy, slow and languid and the zig-zag of lightning
- rain storm – direct spatial pattern – sudden, fine touch, staccato
- sunshine – spherical, radiant, warmth
- shadows and reflective images in water pools.

Drama will be based on stories and poems about how the people, animals and plants are affected by different weather conditions.

At Key Stage 2 as children's depth of geographical understanding grows they are able to conceptualise about important issues which, in addition to discussion and written analysis, can be portrayed through the arts especially through dramatic dialogue expressing differing viewpoints. As their geographical vocabulary extends children are able to conceptualise on a much larger scale, understanding about changes in temperature, the effects of global warming, transport, industry, power and vegetation. Population migration, increase and depopulation can all be communicated through the arts. Physical and human processes can be understood through enactment, for example, the effects of flooding, factory closures, urban decay and regeneration. The impact of events that have shaped and changed people's lives and their responses to them provide stimuli and content for the arts, whether in the form of songs, cantatas, dances, playlets or through visual forms. Figure 6.7 is a group shape in dance showing the patterns of land formations using arms, wrists, hands and fingers.

Figure 6.7   Dance group of children using hands to depict choreographic form based on landforms.

The relationship of humankind and geographical environment is epitomised in the way in which outdoor adventures and the various challenges presented by nature have symbolised human achievement and conquest. The story of crossing Antarctica and the trials and tribulations of climbing mountains fire the imagination and can be used as stimuli for the arts. References to accounts of climbing Mount Everest provide a resource bank of ideas to be used based on the conditions of the mountainous environment and the ways in which men and women have responded to them. The following ideas, which are appropriate for Key Stage 2, incorporate two contrasting approaches – one depicting the physical environment and the other the human responses to it.

Everest expedition

Creating the environment through voice, music and movement in performance and in the use of materials in visual art will mean examining the physical features of the mountainous territory. This will involve learning the vocabulary, defining the physical features and matching them with four types of language – verbal (poetry, prose words of description and metaphor), musical (sounds and instruments that evoke the atmosphere of the landform), kinaesthetic (the space patterns expressed through the body, the shape expressed individually, in pairs and in groups) and visual (the line, volume, texture, pattern, form as expressed through materials and media).

Scene 1

Ice in the mountains – create a glacial sculpture of the landscape. This can include glacial sheets, ice-tongues, angular rock fragments, sharp sand, pinnacles, pyramidal peaks, corries (scalloped shape), trough, basin, rock-steps, ridges and hanging valleys. Contrast the shapes of valley sections – V- and U-shaped sections. Consider the movement of ice – slow-moving, rasping, advancing, receding.

Scene 2

Mountain adventure; this scene considers how the people respond to the mountain. Scenes can include those based on famous expeditions of the past, such as the conquest of Everest, the crossing of Antarctica or crossing the Andes.

Religious education

The Holy Bible is rich in inspirational stories and imagery that can be celebrated through the arts. These include the story of Moses, Noah and the flood, Job's Dream, the Psalms, the Nativity, the Parables of Jesus and the Easter story. The Christian story of Creation can be given imaginative treatment in the arts, as can other creation stories found in a number of the world's cultures which have inspired many generations of artists. Fashioning model animals in clay appeals to very young children who delight in thinking up interesting studies and learning the names and shapes of a wide number of animals, insects, reptiles and birds. Observance and worship expressed through the arts can be linked to the major British festivals which are celebrated in various forms throughout the country and which are based on religions or folk traditions. They include the Christian festivals of Advent, Christmas, Lent, and Easter, the Jewish festival of Rosh Hashanah, the Chinese New Year, the Scottish Hogmanay, the Muslim celebration of Eid, the Hindu/Sikh festival of Diwali, and traditional celebrations of Bonfire Night, Hallowe'en, and May Day. This section will consider a number of integrated arts approaches.

Space Christmas

Space Christmas presents the main elements of the Christmas story set in a space world of the future. Space kings will make the journey through the universe, using space craft as their means of travel. The scenario, based on mime, percussion, voice narrative, choral speaking and improvised dialogue is as follows.

Scene 1

Advent – use a movement and mime motif based on awaiting and searching. Include looking through windows, doors, viewing platforms and telescopes. Conclude with a class tableau showing three space ships, each conveying a king. For the sound accompaniment, children can write their own story based on biblical text, which can be read or recited with a background sound of electronic music or percussion composition.

Scene 2

This depicts the birth of the Saviour in a run-down space station. There is rejoicing, as space angels and kings travel through light-years to bring gifts and to worship. The shepherds are robots, and, working in groups of three, devise a simple, repetitive task, for example mechanical actions, such as lifting, carrying, putting down, as loading or unloading movements. They become still as the Messenger Angel comes and conveys the glad tidings. Space robots travel in threesomes towards the space station where they pay homage to the Christ Child. Sound accompaniment will follow the same format as in the previous scene.

Scene 3

Flight across the universe – this tells of the terror of Herod's anger and wrath as represented by a space tyrant, and the fear of the holy family as they flee to safety. The holy family will escape from the space station and board a space craft. Children represent the space ship. Herod is a space tyrant and symbolises evil – use a distinctive voice and movement to convey the power of a space king that ultimately is eclipsed by the spiritual power of the Christ Child.

Scene 4

Universal peace – this final scene conveys the message of Christian peace and goodwill and takes the notion of peace on earth to be a universal, timeless ideal. Use movement and voice to convey harmony of the spheres, with children working as individuals, with partners and in groups, depicting a view of the universe based on the revolutions and pathways of planets. Use percussion or electronic accompaniment at the start of the scene slowing down until everyone is still. Use voices – silence at the beginning, with whispers and then voices becoming audible and louder as the movement slows down and stops. Use a collage of word sounds and phrases that depict the message of peace and goodwill.

A Christmas of today, using contemporary resources can also use the principal elements of the Christian message. It may relate to the plight of the lowly and often forgotten peoples of the trouble spots of the world today or be a presentation on how Christmas is celebrated by children throughout the world. Folk-art of different cultures can provide the stimulus for work with children, including the singing of carols from other lands and the dramatisation of folk-stories. The evergreen plants – holly, ivy, spruce and pine – each tell their own story, and many pagan rites were incorporated into Christmas festivals. In England, one of the finest examples of custom is the incorporation of the mummers' play into traditional celebrations. Old plays, handed down from generation to generation, contain colourful uses of dialogue, costumes and masks and are full of humour.

The interrelated curriculum mode allows teachers the choice of subject matter for the arts area, fitting in with the specific areas of study of respective areas of the National Curriculum 2000. The teaching method in all cases follows the same pattern as explained in Chapter 1 and as developed in the four chapters relating to the drama, dance, music and visual art modes. The concluding chapter, 'Professional Growth', considers the means by which teachers can develop their teaching of the integrated arts in the primary school.

CHAPTER 7

Professional Growth

THE CREATIVE APPROACH TO TEACHING AND LEARNING THE ARTS

Professional growth is the means by which teachers gain confidence in teaching the arts effectively, achieve an understanding of the inherent principles that inform their best practice and, through self- and peer analysis, discover how to extend their own abilities. It advances and strengthens the teaching of the arts in the primary school thereby improving their status. The creative approach to teaching and learning in and through the arts requires that teachers and children are empowered by a variety of skills that facilitate the progression, development and expression of ideas that finally materialise as artifacts. The pedagogical principles that inform teaching and learning strategies ensure that:

- children become proficient in the intrinsic skills of each artistic discipline – drama, dance, music and visual art
- children apply these skills creatively in both single discipline and integrated contexts by producing a variety of artifacts
- children acquire critical understanding of the processes involved and the nature of their own artifacts
- children acquire critical understanding of their own work and that of other artists in a variety of contexts.

The teaching and learning framework for the arts as presented in Chapter 1 and developed in subsequent chapters requires professional strategies that relate to the four learning experiences as outlined above, perceived in relation to the whole curriculum. This will ensure that children experience harmonious and unified learning experiences, derived from the synergy that takes place between the arts and with other areas of study within the primary school curriculum.

DEVELOPING NEW TEACHING COMPETENCES

Teaching integrated arts in the primary school is the application of belief and theory acquired through teachers' personal engagement as artists with hands-on/minds-on experience with children in school. Teachers' self-belief and attitude towards the arts will determine individual personal practice within the school's policy and, equally important, a general sense of value and encouragement by society. In the nationally legislated arts programme there is the expectancy that the arts can be taught, and there is a need to know which methods are the most successful. Decision-making and how teachers make judgements inevitably informs their teaching.

There is a clear methodology when it comes to the planning, implementation, evaluation and assessment of the process of teaching the arts, aspects of which will focus on the main areas of learning within the programmes of study and attainment targets. There are two main issues at stake:

1. The teacher's evaluation of the way in which children respond in the arts. This includes formative and summative assessment of process and product and is based on the way in which children progress and achieve.
2. The teacher's evaluation of his/her own performance in relation to how the children respond in the arts. This is based upon personal teaching approaches and competences in relation to the formative and summative assessment of children's learning processes and the qualities of the artifacts they produce.

Pedagogically, teachers need to ask five key questions:

- What is the relationship between what I teach and the achievements of the children?
- What is the relationship between how I teach and the achievement of the children?
- How can I improve on my teaching in relation to points 1 and 2?
- What do I perceive as my areas of strength and why?
- What do I perceive as the area requiring improvement and why?

These questions will relate to the four main areas of understanding in the arts – the acquisition of skills in each arts area, the processes and production of art works, the critical understanding and the cultural context.

Intellectual monitoring and analysis of taught sessions depends upon the sensory perceptions of individual teachers. In drama, dance and visual art, the visual aspects of what is taking place provides the major tool of analysis, whereas in music and drama, aural analysis of what is taking place is important. Overall, the effective and sensitive use of voice, the response clues, the facial expression, non-verbal communication, gesture and clarity of verbal responses are utilised in order that individual teaching style and class interaction are brought into play. In integrated arts sessions, there is an amalgamation of these skills that permit informed enquiry and response.

The three-stage planning process, as outlined in the introductory chapter, from overview, medium- and short-term engagement means that teachers begin with some idea of the final outcome because they analyse the anticipated artistic content to determine what the children need to learn (skills). Such skills are systematically taught as part of the learning programme that provides children with the means (skills) for their creative expression. The practical application, based on this teaching and learning structural framework, accommodates individual interpretation and is designed to facilitate creativity. The intended outcome is based upon a professional vision that, while recognising the tried routes and pathways that lead to the achievement of goals, also encourages and promotes experimental and novel procedures. According to personal abilities, teachers will demonstrate and use children to demonstrate, as well as using explanation to expand and develop ideas. Irrespective of the nature of the art forms that the children create, they will each have their own unique identity, and will reflect the stage in their creative and cultural growth. Children learn a great deal from each other and for each activity there will be pace setters.

Understanding about the quality of teaching means knowing what to expect of children and how to improve or maintain standards. Teachers observe the works of art that are exhibited or performed by the children, whether paintings, dances, dramatic presentations, musical compositions or presentations in the integrated mode, and will then form personal judgements about what they have seen. Making judgements about children's work and any assessment of it is integral to the taught programme and, although the teacher is ultimately responsible for summative assessment, the evaluation of children's work is interactive between children and their teachers in so far as discussion and formation of opinion is concerned.

The following statements represent the nature of the teacher's thought processes when making a critical evaluation of children's art work:

- What do I see/hear? – Analysis of the art form in terms of overall visual/aural impact.
- How do I respond to what I see/hear? – Personal interpretation and understanding of the painting, dance, play or musical composition.
- How does the artifact convey its meaning to me? – Understanding how the children have used the materials in a particular way to communicate effectively their ideas and feelings.
- What is my opinion of what I see? – Making an evaluative judgement of the artifact in educational terms of development, standard and expectation.
- How did I arrive at this opinion? – Understanding the reasons for my choice based on criteria of judgement.
- Which aspect especially appeals to me and why? – Recognition of both the good and weaker qualities.
- How can I build upon the children's strengths? – Devise a teaching strategy that incorporates a learning plan for the children.
- How can I overcome the children's weaknesses? – Devise a teaching strategy that incorporates a learning plan for the children.

Discussion of work between teachers and children is part of the teaching and learning process and through interactive dialogue of this nature, children acquire the meta-language that is used to support modes of learning. Intervention points within the entire process of the artistic experience occur when children and teachers are able to discuss work, either in progress or at the final stage of showing and sharing.

A further way of building up professional confidence is to comprehend that critical understanding of the arts incorporates the critical understanding and ongoing evaluative processes that are inherent within the art of teaching. Self-questioning about intention and output, process and problem-solving stages have direct application to works of art, since there is a relationship between the act of synthesis and the act of analysis, both in terms of the method and purpose of producing artifacts, and of the methods and processes that refine pedagogical practice. This applies to all the arts and requires that teachers understand how the technical aspects of an art form facilitate creative expression, and how the final stage is the communication of the ideas and feelings as contained within the artifact. The artifact as the culmination of the production stage contains within its form, artistic knowledge. The response that the artifact engenders relates to the appreciation and interpretation of the artifact, and is based on a creative response of a critical nature. While common, shared experiences exist, the worth of individual responses and reasons for them are also valued. This means that having an opinion and coming to a judgement are skills that can be taught, but not by prescription and not necessarily in the expectation of acquiring consensus. Understanding about formulating criteria for judgement, whether in terms of what to look for in the received work or in the child's own artifact, is fundamental to meaningful teaching.

The following guidelines are not definitive and are intended only to provide a structural framework from which teachers can develop their own criteria. Individual comment is mostly directed at individual level, but it has to be recognised that a great deal of the work the children do in the primary school will be part of partner or small group projects. Making judgements about children's art work is about making educational as well as artistic judgements, and when criteria are being formulated attitude, progress and achievement are likely to be included. The Record of Achievement (Figure 1.9, p. 17), records the knowledge, skills and understanding under the four areas of creative process, creative communication, critical understanding and contextual understanding. These areas can be further subdivided to include criteria reference points as outlined below which include statements based on attitude, and educational progress relating to work methods and artistic achievement:

- Creative process – the pupil's response to art-making. This section includes comment about individual attitude towards the arts; attitude towards self; progress made in drama, dance, music and visual art in terms of the acquisition of skills based on the observation of children's performance in their lessons.
- Creative communication – the nature of work produced. This section includes comment about individual achievement in terms of the completed works in drama, dance, music and visual art. It will make evaluative comment on performance and presentation of work in terms of the meaning and content of the artifact, and the impact, technical quality and aesthetic aspects of the work. Evidence is based on the evaluation of what the children have achieved – the dances, paintings, puppets, playlets, songs, musical pieces which they have composed.
- Critical understanding – pupil's response to their own work and that of peers. This section includes comment about children's critical responses to their own work and of others, and will use as evidence what the child has said in conversation with the teacher during practical sessions, during group discussion sessions and through written evidence. Remarks will convey whether children use vocabulary well, whether they are descriptive in their comment or make evaluative statements in their response, determining what they see, hear, and feel about art works and how they comprehend the meaning of art works which they and their peers have produced.
- Contextual understanding – discussion and writing about art works. This section includes comment about children's critical responses to art works within specific cultural contexts and will be based on the evidence of discussion and writing. Remarks will convey whether children use vocabulary well, whether they are descriptive or evaluative in what they say or write, with comments that are more than preferences of liking or disliking, but are supported with evidence.

Assessment is an ongoing process that is an integral part of the learning programme in the arts both at formative and summative stages. It is important to consider the manner in which assessment helps to develop the teaching of art and how it can improve the children's conceptual understanding about what they do and see.

Self-evaluation used by teachers is based on intention, outcome and standard of work produced by the children, set in the context and belief that nothing short of a maximum response is expected from the children, and that assessment of their work is applied sensitively in a positive manner. Work methods and outcomes are individual, both in terms of children's work and the teacher's style. Teachers establish and develop a particular approach which is based on their relationships with the children, linked with their understanding of what they know and understand about the arts. In terms of specific lessons, it is important to question how well each part of the lesson went and how the intention matched the abilities of the individual needs of the pupils.

What should teachers look for in the evaluation of children's work? To reiterate points related to the reporting and recording of children's achievements in the arts, teachers require be aware of the thoughtful manner in which the children engaged in the activity, the perceived understanding and the progress made through doing and then discussing. Their understanding is then expressed through assessment and reporting. The outcome of children's efforts will be causal, and many questions will be raised by the teacher such as:

- Did the children engage successfully in their work?
- How independent were the children in the ways in which they concentrated, controlled and produced their work?
- Were the children concentrating on what they were doing?
- Did the children make efforts to develop their skills?
- Did the children show independence in decision-making?
- Did children work well with each other?

Judgements about technical aspects of specific art forms and ongoing decision-making reflects the understanding of the child's relationship between skill acquisition and how they were used in the art-making process. These are important factors in understanding the nature of teaching creativity in a creative way. Helping individual children to 'draw out' their perceptions and then supporting them as they attempt to crystallise ideas within a symbolic art statement is the teacher's role.

It follows logically that the type of observation, interaction, clarity of aims and objectives as outlined above necessitate an ongoing assessment process recording the children's progress and achievement. The kind of questions, the manner of intervention, and the nature of the discussion all provide the means of extending the quality of both teaching and learning. As previously mentioned in an earlier chapter, children's progress can be recorded at intervals as required by the school, based on observational notes relating to work undertaken within each project and consolidated each term. The important aspects to note are the children's operational skills of art-making, their achievements in work produced, their critical understanding of the operational skills and their understanding of the cultural aspects of art. The teacher's comment will relate to professional judgement based on evidence set against specific criteria and based on a five-point scale ranging from children who are highly confident, those who give very good or good responses, to those whose work is acceptable. Some children may be under-performing and reasons and remedies must be sought. Some children may lack motivation and require extra encouragement, while others may have particular difficulties, perhaps in the acquisition of specific skills or in gaining the confidence to apply the skills more creatively – these children will require specific support.

ISSUES AND VALUES IN TEACHING THE INTEGRATED ARTS

The methods advocated in this book for teaching integrated arts in the primary school are both coherent and developmental and children's progression is closely linked with the teacher's understanding of the nature of artistic engagement and the elements within it. The foundation of arts teaching rests on the way in which teachers are successful in enabling children to understand the arts. This implies an understanding on the part of the teacher not only of the arts themselves but also how to teach the arts and children's responses to the arts. Although these attributes derive from knowing about the arts in school generally and their place and role within the curriculum, they are underpinned by a secure knowledge of each separate arts mode. The key to success in teaching the integrated arts is knowing how parameters and boundaries are interconnected rather than being mutually exclusive. They are gained through personal involvement at a practical level – engaging in the type of activities involving the children as well as practical experiences in the classroom – supported by theoretical understanding. In this way successful and improved practice is achieved relating to the developmental stages in the child's artistic growth, which will encompass chronological age, intellectual, emotional and physical development. The application of the principles of good practice in teaching the arts means that teachers will demonstrate in the classroom the relationship of educational theory and teaching practice by a clear understanding of what is intended and why. The following key areas will be covered in a reflexive way:

- a good balance in the relationship between teaching technique and creativity
- a clear definition of the teacher's role as facilitator of the arts using creative teaching approaches that offer security to children
- a clear definition of the child's role in experiencing the arts in relation to peers/teacher and received works
- an effective use of resources and materials by teachers and children.

The teacher's role in meeting requirements and facilitating learning in these key areas is intended to develop the children's confidence in each area of study. The nurturing of creativity arises from the appropriate environment that is conducive to imaginative, sensitive and artistic development. Strength and confidence in teaching the arts is reflected in the ethos of the school, especially where staff support each other and when they are provided with positive leadership.

THE TEACHING AND LEARNING ENVIRONMENT FOR THE ARTS

A visitor, upon entering a school where the arts are clearly considered to be a vital ingredient in the education of the children, is immediately impressed by the external signs that communicate an active engagement in an arts based philosophy within the school. It might be the stimulating visual environment of exhibitions and display areas relating to the nature of work within the school. It might be the glimpse of children at work in classroom, hall, or designated work area, or perhaps the sound of music, or the sight of children researching information in the library, or using the computer. It might be the day when there is a presentation to an audience, or it might be on the occasion when children are working with an artist in education.

A parent with a child attending a school where the arts really do matter might well be impressed with the overall ambience and pervading atmosphere that encourages creativity, individual aspiration and the sharing of success among the pupils. Many parents are drawn into providing support for the school and enjoy being actively involved in a way that encourages the arts and adds further quality to the corporate life of the school. A school governor cannot fail to notice the way in which the artistic life of the school thrives and blossoms out into the wider neighbourhood and community, and a head teacher will gain personal satisfaction from the way in which the creative life of the school enhances the quality of the academic and social life as a whole, especially when it permeates the teaching style of other areas of the curriculum.

Establishing a secure teaching and learning environment for the arts as part of the corporate life of a school requires a clear policy for the arts that promotes enthusiastic team work and leadership, characterised by professional dedication that generates self-confidence for both the staff and children. By giving the arts a high profile, the people who belong to the school are also given a high profile – this is important in making people feel that they matter and are achieving the highest standards.

An audit is a practical way to ensure a stimulating teaching and learning environment that is conducive to the development of the arts. Identify strengths and weaknesses of the entire school and use this information to devise the fourth 'R' policy, thereby reaffirming the arts curriculum in the primary school as presented in Chapter 1 (see Fig. 1.1, p. 2). At this stage, a school will find ways of improving its provision for the arts, whether it relates to the improvement of existing dedicated spaces for arts teaching or the specific locations and facilities for art, dance, music and drama. Building up resources, storage areas, wardrobe, installation of spot lights, re-examining the floor surface, location of display boards, discussing ways of using artists in education, making the best use of outside visits – all these factors help to strengthen the investment in human capital, that is the staff and children.

A stimulating environment is vital to creative teaching – it whets the appetite and satisfies artistic hunger. It is lively rather than passive, proactive rather than reactive, responsive rather than dismissive, interactive rather than didactic, organised rather than chaotic, targeted rather than haphazard, but always alert and open to chance happening and momentary inspirations. It is sympathetic towards dreaming and visualising, scornful towards prescription, nurturing towards wisdom and sharing, respectful of individual viewpoint. Down-to-earth aspects help to generate the intellectual environment, the thought processes and the way in which the children derive enjoyment from the lifestyle within the school. An inspirational teaching and learning environment for the arts generates the creative wealth of a school. Children attending a school where the arts matter accept the arts as an extension of themselves. Not only do they discover an important part of themselves through the arts, but they also learn a great deal about other children.

CHILDREN'S PERSONAL, SOCIAL AND MORAL DEVELOPMENT IN THE ARTS

Over many generations and in numerous societies throughout the world, the arts have been used as vehicles through which children have become culturally aware. The discipline of the arts and the long process involved in acquiring artistry in music, dance, drama and visual art were used as powerful civilising influences on children, marking their stages of childhood growth, not only giving them the manners and attributes expected of childhood, but also preparing them for the accomplishments of adulthood. There are some children today benefiting from the various forms of extra-mural tuition in the arts, supported either by their parents or by sessions provided by local education authorities (LEAs). Notwithstanding, it is the responsibility of primary school teachers to take on board their highly significant role as instigators of learning, responding to the needs of children through their personal, social and moral development in the arts, so that every child can have the special excitement and enjoyment that active engagement in the arts can bring. Everyday schooling, arts clubs and societies endorse this.

The National Curriculum 2000 offers non-statutory guidelines on the knowledge, skills and understanding attributed to personal, social and health education (PSHE). It is both possible and desirable for primary school teachers to use the arts as a means through which children learn to understand the meaning of the various aspects of PSHE. At Key Stage 1 experiences in dance, drama, music and visual art will enable children to develop confidence as they acquire artistic skills and apply them creatively. They will gain in their self-responsibility as they discover their own abilities in these areas and recognise their own achievements. The arts, as effective modes of learning, develop aesthetic sensibilities that enable very young children to come to terms with themselves emotionally. They communicate their own feelings through their art work and also learn how to interpret the feelings of other artists. In performance, they gain understanding of different types of emotion through enactment, and in dance they understand the meaning of healthy, physical expression. Personal responsibilities as citizens can be learned by being artists, discussing and capturing important issues within a particular art work, and also through the nature of the behaviour required in practical sessions – dance, drama and music in particular require courteous behaviour. Mutual respect and self-discipline are acquired, vital to children's learning of how to develop good relationships and respect for people.

At Key Stage 2 the arts continue to have a powerful impact upon children's PSHE development, helping them to build up confidence levels and providing opportunities to experience responsibility. At this stage, some children become despondent when they realise that their academic achievements do not match those of their friends, and often find compensation and personal satisfaction from their achievements in the arts. They see the arts as a means of communicating their thoughts about important issues affecting not only their lives but also those of other people in the world. The content of the arts programme can effectively relate to aspects of citizenship, especially when it enables children to reflect on moral, social and cultural issues using the arts in an integrated manner to focus on a particular issue. Reference to exemplars in previous chapters will show how each can be evaluated from a PSHE perspective. The responsibilities and knowledge pertaining to healthier and safer lifestyles can be considered through the arts, with children using factual information and resources provided by the teacher as a basis of their art work. Posters, plays, dances, and songs convey messages in a convincing and

memorable way. Older children can spend time compiling th
performance work for presentation to others. The school assemt
such activities. Children as artists, having mutual respect for each oᵥ
of each other's work, continue to develop the social ambience tᵥ
lessons, showing greater degrees of subtlety as they approach Year 6
relationships and having respect for others is implicit in the way in ᵥ
taught, and endorses the significant role the arts play at Key Stage 2 in eᵥ
to gain insight into the complexities of social and moral values.

The arts are also means of expressing worship, and in certain contexts prᵒ ᵥ children
with the means for their spiritual development. This can happen in a number of ways. As
modes of communication, the arts can be used for examining and presenting moral and
religious issues, either as part of religious education or in school assembly. A different
usage is when the arts convey the spirit and meaning of worship through dance, music, or
dramatic liturgy with the sincerity and conviction of prayer, perhaps as part of the
school's religious assembly or as a special celebration in church. Through song, dance,
music, and drama children can take part in organised ceremonies of Christian or inter-
faith worship.

Many people, including children, derive a special or 'peak' experience when engaging
in the arts. For some this can be likened to a spiritual experience, for others it is a personal
experience and awareness of the 'inner-self', a feeling of great joy or of a deeper medita-
tive nature that is secular rather than religious. The metaphysical aspect of arts education
is of immeasurable value.

EFFECTS AND EFFECTIVENESS OF THE ARTS

In examining the effects and the effectiveness of the arts it is necessary to ask two fundamental questions: what can the arts offer to children and what can children offer the arts?

Children's engagement in the arts has a twofold effect. Firstly, there is the belief that
the study of the arts is beneficial, that to be devoid of it is to be disadvantaged. Running
parallel to this is the belief that children who receive a good education in the arts will in
turn provide the initiative and leadership that will fuel future development. Committed
teaching of the integrated arts in the primary school guarantees high quality aesthetic and
creative experiences offered through the arts curriculum and determines the distinctiveness of children's cultural life. Academic performance is enhanced as individual achievement is enhanced and within children a lifelong interest in the arts is kindled. The
teaching approaches and learning exemplars in previous chapters demonstrate the way in
which independent linear programmes of study in the main subject areas of dance, drama,
music and visual art are interpreted and developed so that the integrative aspects are
conjoined into unified teaching and learning experiences. In Chapter 6 the holistic nature
of learning was emphasised, and demonstrated how children bring distinctive modes of
thinking into a special related focus or topic which is researched from the perspective of
other curriculum areas. The arts are used to reinforce learning, to build and strengthen
children's confidence, self-esteem and self-respect.

Art works contain within their meaning statements that reflect the value system of the
artist who created the work. In school, children's engagement in the arts will often bring

face to face with established value systems. The National Forum for Values in Education and the Community (May 1997) published a consensus of values which can be used by schools and teachers to inform their practice (DfEE & QCA 1999: 147–9). The statement of values pertaining to the self, relationships and responsibilities, society, and the environment, can be interpreted to support the way in which the arts are inextricably linked with the value systems of society, either challenging or reflecting upon them.

The programmes of study at Key Stages 1 and 2 in the primary school, when effectively taught and resourced, permit all children to develop their own personal accomplishments in drama, dance, music and visual art, at practical and critical levels, irrespective of background, preparing them to move on with confidence to work at Key Stage 3 and the greater challenges of the secondary school. The arts education received in the primary school not only provides the foundation from which future work will blossom as children's education progresses through adolescence and into adulthood, but provides the vital link between one generation and the next.

Each generation discovers its own cultural and artistic style and experienced teachers will talk about the way in which different cohorts of children they have taught have responded uniquely and individually to the way in which they have expressed their ideas, whether through visual art or in the performing arts. The values that children develop in their youth will inform them in their adulthood, and these values will often be reasserted through art works and the responses to them. Young children are in possession of a great creative zest, both in terms of the novelty of their ideas and the passion of their feeling. The creative teacher will be sensitive to the children's needs and will always be mindful of the excitement of providing the channel through which these creative ideas will flow. The children's own contribution to the arts is like the flame of an ever-burning torch – it illuminates the future even though it was kindled in the past by previous generations. A high quality education in and through the arts provided in the primary school is the way in which society invests in the future.

EQUAL OPPORTUNITIES AND INDIVIDUAL NEEDS THROUGH THE ARTS

Provision for equality and meeting individual needs through the arts in the primary school is enshrined in the national framework and purposes of the National Curriculum 2000 (The school curriculum and the National Curriculum: values, aims and purposes), requiring that all maintained schools provide a balanced and broadly based curriculum that promotes the children's spiritual, moral, cultural, mental and physical development as part of the process that prepares them for the responsibilities and opportunities of their adult experience. The national framework, which includes the National Curriculum and religious education, not only enables schools to meet the needs of all pupils but encourages them to develop their distinctive qualities based on the ethos of the communities they serve. Cultural diversity in the arts curriculum is celebrated through the choice of content of what children dance, paint, act or make music about, as exemplars in previous chapters have indicated. Not only do the arts reflect specific cultures, but the way in which the arts are used creatively can help to clarify the meanings and values of other cultures. These will be realised within the school itself, especially in areas where children come from different cultural backgrounds. It will remain within the domain of every primary school to seek ways of sharing and making partnerships through the arts at local, national and international levels. Exchange days, when work is presented, or when children work together with visiting artists are possibilities, as well as communicating using technological means, thereby highlighting the interrelationship of artistic cultures at local, national and global levels. Teachers and schools can take the initiative to discover and utilise cultural symbols as a means of making links through the arts. There are a number of successful projects that have or are taking place, as for example the Endeavour Project which resulted in cultural celebrations and exchanges between children in Whitby, England, Fremantle, Australia and Vancouver, Canada, arising from the performance of English country dances on board HMB *Endeavour*.

The National Curriculum 2000 facilitates that all children, whatever their background or aptitude, have the ability to express themselves successfully through the arts. Teaching integrated arts in the primary school following the suggested methods recognises the importance of each individual and the teaching approaches take account of children's wide-ranging abilities, especially in relation to the acquisition of skills where some children may encounter difficulties while others display special gifts. The arts are the means of breaking down the formal boundaries of achievement and under-achievement in tested academic areas, since all children are empowered by the use of their imagination and the ability to express themselves emotionally through the arts, often achieving sensitivity and poignancy in their work. The creative and sensitive teacher will have the insight to ensure that all needs are met, that children in the same class have the opportunity of working with each other in the arts, so that strengths are shared for the common good. The knowledge, skills and understanding of the arts programme is accessible to all and promotes individual challenge, development and achievement.

RESOURCING THE ARTS

Children and their teachers are the most valuable resource base for the arts but to receive and provide high quality teaching children and teachers require to be supported by an adequate resource base. At a minimum level this means:

- space for activities to be undertaken safely with access to hall space for dance, drama, music and flexible use of classroom space for drama and music
- working areas for art, within or adjacent to classrooms, providing a wet area with a non-slip floor
- equipment and materials for art with suitable storage facilities
- musical instruments, small properties required in dance and drama including a small wardrobe of costumes
- display space for art materials in the classroom and about the school
- electrical equipment – tape-recorders, CD players, video camera and recorder, computers with Internet/Intranet connection
- funding for visits and for children to work with professional artists
- funding for continuing professional development of staff
- library collection of books about the arts
- library collection of music
- a collection of visual art works and artifacts, original and reproduction items.

Teachers will make use of the above resources in a number of different ways, often selecting examples in order to interest and motivate children into creating their own work. However, it is also important to select more difficult pieces that challenge children's thinking about art. Artifacts are used to enhance children's understanding of the use of materials and processes and to stimulate their own creativity. Learning to use and interpret familiar subject matter, or learning how to express ideas by using a particular painting as a reference point encourages critical discussion. Received works can also be used as a means of extending the children's knowledge of the technical and aesthetic aspects about the use of colour, pattern and texture, line and tone, shape, form and space of art works. Resources to support the teaching of the arts are increasing, but some areas still require further materials.

BEYOND THE CLASSROOM – WORKING WITH PROFESSIONAL ARTISTS

Theatre in education, dance in education and music in education groups, some of which are attached to orchestras as well as individual visual artists and individual performing artists, offer their services to schools and provide an expertise in many specialist and cultural areas. International companies visit schools, bringing speciality performances of dance, drama, musical instruments and colour costume. Whether African dancing and drumming or Malaysian puppet theatre, the experiences offered are both unique and memorable. Working with artists in their own school holds real benefits for the children, and partnership policies with professional companies and providers from major cultural organisations as well as locally based and community-driven projects will further enhance the children's experience of the arts. Partnership experiences also extend the artistic understanding of teachers and can provide mutual benefits for the artists if they utilise the wealth of the teacher's expertise in understanding how children learn and respond. Equally, when artists provide stimulating, innovative ideas that elicit novel responses from the children, they too are supporting teachers in their professional growth.

To make maximum use of the experience advanced preparation is advisable, so that clear expectations on the part of school and artist are understood, and to ensure that the experience is integrated within the planned programme of learning.

BEYOND THE CLASSROOM – DISCOVERING THE CREATIVE ENVIRONMENT

Resourcing the arts effectively means providing children with inspirational experiences that extend beyond the immediate classroom and into the external environment. This can be achieved through virtual and real means so that children can benefit from the treasures offered by museums, art galleries and heritage sites. These are symbols of the nation's cultural wealth and can provide a powerful resource for the arts and make immediately accessible the integration with history, geography, science and technology. Museum and gallery education officers are important agents in developing work in the area of critical and contextual studies and the knowledge and information they impart will also act as a creative springboard for teachers. Museums are educational institutions in their own right, making purposeful provision through the items they display and the programmes and publications they provide. As a public educational resource there are numerous opportunities for development if schools can forge partnerships with their local museum and plan activities that integrate with the main programmes of learning in the arts. Depending upon locality and accessibility it is desirable to have a particular focus for each visit made, for example, looking at ceramic design and using it as a stimulus for an integrated arts project. If museums have sufficient space, a return visit can be made so that children can present their work.

The interpretation of heritage is a further aspect of the arts portfolio. Heritage sites are often visited by primary school children and some offer educational programmes and living history events that complement the requirements of the National Curriculum. Links between the site and specific integrated learning programmes in the arts can be planned and put into practice. Examples of integrated activities in previous chapters have direct application to selected sites, when for example, the performance of a masque is appropriate. Heritage as a teaching resource can be used at the commencement of an integrated arts project, or as the culmination if it is possible for children to use the location as a performance venue. Activities of a practical nature will require negotiation with owners and custodians.

During the summer months the outdoor environment is ideal for teaching purposes. It may be the immediate location of the school grounds but there are outdoor heritage centres located in parklands or forests which provide stimuli for the arts. When organising outings, many schools will benefit from voluntary help from parents and other responsible adults who are able to work under the supervision of the teachers.

DEVELOPING PROFESSIONAL COMPETENCES FOR ARTS TEACHING

Teachers can inform their own practice and are able to monitor their own teaching progress as it relates to the experiences they instigate for the children. The acquisition and development of new teaching competences in the manner described at the beginning of this chapter will provide the day-to-day operational practices in the classroom, but as professional experiences and opportunities develop then new challenges arise and the already competent teacher will want to progress, take on more responsibilities, develop new arts initiatives, help less experienced colleagues, or engage in some form of recognised research based teaching in the arts. Observing other teachers in action, taking part in and leading discussions with colleagues, looking at and talking about children's work and experimenting with new ideas, will be supported by reading about artists and their work and publications about the arts in school. Organising practical workshops, developing partnership schemes by arranging visits to galleries or theatres, and cultivating personal interest in the arts with children will entail embarking upon further research to understand how individual children perceive the arts – what they see, hear, and feel – in relation to observed progress.

The teaching and learning framework for the integrated arts as presented in Chapter 1, values the major knowledge areas and their interrelationship and accords equal value to the artifact and the processes undertaken in its realisation. It is not dominated by any idealist assumptions that as the art process is unique to the individual that in itself is sufficient to define practice. The framework encourages an interactive dialogue between teachers and children which facilitates freedom of expression as a form of personal creativity, valued because it conjoins reason with feeling – the two indivisible components of artistic practice. Sensitive and imaginative teaching is of paramount importance, drawing out children's own ideas and nurturing their creative growth, ultimately to provide them with intellectual and emotional fulfilment.

In developing an understanding of the context of art it is not necessary to produce artifacts that are culturally determined – artifacts should celebrate art work and be used to inform creativity and critical appreciation. Knowing about existing art works is a means of fuelling ideas for the future. Equally, it is both possible and desirable to verbalise about the arts. This happens in both critical and creative contexts, since it is in the classroom and hall when children are actively engaged that they acquire practical meaning to verbal language, and when viewing and listening to art works that they apply their own experiences of language in critical contexts. Self-monitoring of professional growth in teaching the arts requires a systematic approach that:

- identifies the area for self-improvement
- devises an ongoing strategy based on mutual discussion with other colleagues in the same or other schools, perhaps linking into a network
- monitors personal progress through the keeping of a personal journal
- moves forward by evaluating the evidence of a journal, children's work and discussion with other colleagues.

MONITORING PROGRESS THROUGH PRACTITIONER BASED ENQUIRY

It is expected that teachers constantly reappraise their teaching and adapt to change, and one of the most appropriate ways of achieving this is to monitor the progress of children and self through practitioner based approaches to teaching in and through the integrated arts. Small, classroom-action arts based projects are viable for teachers of Reception to Key Stages 1 and 2. They allow teachers to experiment by recording their own actions, thoughts and feelings, responding to the way in which they teach an aspect of the arts curriculum, selected because of the desire for personal improvement. If possible it is helpful to elicit help from at least one other colleague or mentor who will act as a critical friend to discuss what happened in a teaching session and how to move forward. Individual teachers can monitor what happens in their teaching by keeping a journal documenting ideas and feelings, perhaps also with a photographic record and/or a tape-recording of work in progress. Exemplars are based on the following strategy:

- identify a particular, personal need or special focus based on teaching/learning experiences
- plan the overview and medium-term view noting the special focus and state how it will be incorporated into the teaching method
- plan the first lesson detailing the intended methods that will highlight the special teaching focus.

Once the first lesson has been taught the evidence should be documented in the notebook and some thought given to it before engaging in a discussion with the critical friend. In considering what happened in relation to the focus area, a decision will be made about how to move on to the next teaching session. This is known as an action step, and reflects the way in which individual teachers respond to their own practice. It may be possible to invite the mentor to observe some of the teaching which is likely to take place for the duration of the project, and for each taught session the same question should be asked: 'How am I improving on my previous practice?' The answer to this question is solved by the implementation of a further series of action steps, each of which signifies progress in professional development.

Pedagogical enquiry that informs good practice in the teaching of the arts will be based on many distinctive areas, and individual teachers will make progress through the collection and interpretation of data related to the action steps which will determine how they are able to improve their own particular practice of teaching the arts. Small-scale self-monitoring will lead to a growth in understanding and enthusiasm that will challenge present assumptions and set up new targets for teaching the integrated arts in the new millennium. As teachers develop in their expertise, it will be possible to emulate the examples of the best practitioners, ensuring access and entitlement to a good quality arts education as being the accepted and expected standard for all children, including partnership links with other agencies.

The promotion of a broad based research approach, examining the principal critical and conceptual issues of teaching the integrated arts, will test how the epistemological teaching and learning framework, as advocated in this book, is being applied in the classroom. Research will also reveal whether the philosophical foundation for teaching integrated arts in the primary school has been realised and whether there has been a concerted effort to ensure that aesthetic and creative education has become the entitlement of every child. The most rewarding discovery will be to find that the nature and quality of the provision of the arts has been successful in determining distinctiveness of cultural life and the academic performance in school. These are the greatest gifts we can give our children at the dawn of the new millennium.

Glossary of Terms

Aesthetic – perceptual qualities which relate to children's personal feelings, attitude and understanding of their own creativity and that of others, which are developed through intellectual, emotional and sensory engagement. Enquiring into the nature of artistic engagement through attempting to explain the nature of the various stages of art processes from making, and realising, to evaluating and appreciating.

Artistic – the ability to make an artifact through selective media forms through which children have conveyed their personal feelings, attitudes and understanding. All children possess artistic ability and express their thoughts and feelings through dance, drama, music and the visual arts.

Assessment – the method by which teachers determine how children are learning and understanding the arts. Formative assessment is used as an ongoing monitoring process, summative assessment marks the end of a specific stage of a learning programme, and will apply to art-making and critical understanding.

Communication – this relates to the two experiences of making and appraising, in the former to the way in which children's ideas, beliefs and feelings are expressed through their art work and in the latter, to the way in which children respond to the artwork of others. In both instances the art form is the vehicle through which ideas and feelings are conveyed and comprehended.

Creative person – children as artists who, through imaginative responses, are capable of producing original work that conveys ideas and feelings through the use of different forms of materials and media in the visual and performing arts.

Creative process – the stages from the inception of children's ideas and the way in which they test the work methods and acquire skills that lead to the production of artifacts, often brought about through a series of problem-solving/solution-seeking strategies.

Creative product – children's artifacts in the form of paintings, sculptures, dances, musical compositions, plays etc., which are the outcomes of the creative process.

Culture – children knowing about human achievement and expression through the arts in different societies throughout the world as representative of a wide range of lifestyles, conditions and value systems. Children are also part of their own culture which will reflect the main values and characteristics of the social and community group to which they belong.

Imagination – children's ability to use their powers of invention and idealisation in tandem with art processes in order to stimulate creativity, thereby producing new ideas and artifacts, whatever the materials and media – dances, compositions, plays, paintings, etc.

Innovation – children's ability to produce that which is new or different from previous art work, by drawing on the powers of the imagination and the technical skills of the specific art forms.

Intended outcome (artistic) – children's ability (with teacher's support) to complete their work.

Intention (artistic) – children's ability (with teacher's support) to have an aim or purpose for a creative task.

Judgement – children's and teachers' ability to form an opinion about art works based on particular criteria.

Multiple intelligences – the theory, expounded by Howard Gardner (1989), of at least seven human intelligences: linguistic, logical-mathematical, spatial, musical, bodily-kinaesthetic, interpersonal and intrapersonal. Gardner helps to explain why children learn, remember, perform and understand in different ways, and promotes the use of decontextualised environments such as museums.

Professional growth – the methods employed by teachers to monitor and inform their own practice of teaching the arts through reappraisal, reflexive practice, and research.

Received works – existing and acknowledged works of art representing different cultures and societies throughout the world, including contemporary works. Music, drama and dance works are brought alive through performance, or are collected as recordings. Visual art works exist in art galleries and museums as originals and are recorded on slides, in books, and electronically. These provide the cultural library for children.

Symbolic form – the metaphorical significance, meaning and feeling contained and conveyed through children's individual art work. Verbal language is a symbolic device, as are other symbol systems including the arts, which as forms of knowledge are conveyed through the organisation of sounds, movements and visual elements. The National Curriculum programmes of study enable children to express themselves and to comprehend a variety of symbol systems in that they are forms through which children learn as well as express ideas of human sensibility.

Traditional arts – arts that exist as part of specific cultures reflecting their historical development and handed down to the present age. Children learn about traditional arts through participation (reconstruction in dance, drama and music), listening and viewing. Traditional arts reflect different social groups and contexts, as for example, court, folk, religious.

Appendix: Resources for the Integrated Arts

DRAMA

A Midsummer Night's Dream, The Kabet Press
All in a Day's Work – *Athletes and Actors*, Heinemann
Beowulf (narrative poem), Oxford University Press
Curtain Up Series of photocopiable plays, A & C Black
Famous People Poster, *William Shakespeare*, Schofield & Simms
Let's Pretend We are … 4+ *Entertainers*, Heinemann
Life and Times, N. Morgan, Wayland
Playtales 6+, Heinemann
Puppet Plays 6+, M. Butterfield, Heinemann
Charlie and the Chocolate Factory, R. Dahl/R. George, Puffin
James and the Giant Peach R. Dahl/R. George, Puffin
Shakespeare for Everyone: *Hamlet, Julius Caesar, Macbeth, The Merchant of Venice, A Midsummer Night's Dream, Romeo and Juliet*, Cherrytree Books, Pearson
Shakespeare's Stories, B. Birch, MacDonald
William Shakespeare, H. Middleton, Oxford
Mr William Shakespeare's Plays 10+, M. Williams, Heinemann
Shakespeare: *The Animated Tales*, L. Garfield, Heinemann
Sound Practice 6–8, A. Parker/J. Stamford, Schofield & Simms
The Oxford Book of Story Poems, Oxford University Press
We're Going on a Bear Hunt, M. Rosen/H.Oxenbury, Heinemann

DANCE

Best Ever Book of Ballet 8+, Heinemann
Ballet, An Usborne Guide
Celebrations in Art – Dance, J. Bright, Magna Books 1996
Daisy, Little Dancer, M. Birkinshaw/D. Pace, Ladybird
Dance, An Usborne Guide
Dances for Tudors and Stuarts (Dolmetsch Historical Dance Society, Secretary, D. Cruickshank, Hunter's Moon, Orcheston, Salisbury, Wiltshire, SP3 4RP)
Masquerade 7+, Heinemann

The Nutcracker, D. Freeman, Pavilion
The World of Ballet 11+, Usborne
Understanding Your Body, Usborne
Starting Ballet, Usborne
Wild Child Multimedia Resources (Bedford Interactive Productions, 19 Edge Road, Thornhill, Dewsbury, WF12 OQA)
The Dance Club 8–11 Six story books about dance, M. Lewis Jones, MacDonald
You Can Do It! 5+ *Dance*, Heinemann
English Folk Dance and Song Society, Cecil Sharp House, 2 Regents Park Road, London NW1 7AY
Hobgoblin Music, 24 Rathbone Place, London W1P 1DG
Primrose Education Resources, White Cross, Lancaster LA1 4XQ

ART

Art in History Series Pack 8+, Heinemann
Art from the Past, Heinemann
Art School 7+, M. Manning/B. Granstrom, Heinemann
Children in Art, J. Anderson, Bracken Books
Design! Fun with Graphics 10+, P. Owen, Belitha Press
Famous People Posters, *Famous Artists*, Schofield & Simms
Getting to Know the World's Greatest Artists, M. Venezia, Children's Press
Magic in Art, A. Sturgis, Belitha Press
Great Artists – Snapping Turtle Guide, Ticktock Publishing Ltd
Masks, J. Mack, British Museum
Masquerade – Schemes of Work for Art in the Primary School, J. Cam, R. Elia and T. Lawlor, Visual Learning Foundation
Primary Art Ages 5–11, R. Clement /S. Page, Longman
Three Primary Video Films, R. Clement, Longman
Focus Ages 5–14 Resources for Visual Education Pack A & B, A. Laing, A. Mcintosh and C. Macqueen, Longman
The Book Project – *Art and Colour Series*, Longman
The History of Western Painting 10+, J. Heslewood, Belitha Press
The History of Western Sculpture 10+, J. Heslewood, Belitha Press
The Life and Work of ... 5+, Heinemann
The Visual Learning Foundation, Robert Blair School, Brewery Road, Islington, London N7 9QJ

MUSIC

Instruments in Music 7+, Heinemann
Classical Music, Jazz and Blues, Rock, Pop and Dance, Folk and Country, World Music, Sound Trackers 10+, Heinemann
Rock n'Roll, 1960s Pop, Reggae, 1970s Pop, Heavy Metal, 1980s Pop

Famous People Posters, *Famous Composers*, Schofield & Simms
Kingfisher Book of Music 10+, Heinemann
Macmillan Compact Music 10+ – history of individual instruments includes audio CD, Macmillan
Making Music Poster, Schofield & Simms
Musical Instruments of the World 5+, B. Carson Turner/J. See, Belitha Press
I Wonder Why? Series, J. Parker, Kingfisher
The Usborne Story of Music, Usborne
First Music – *Recorder, Keyboard, Piano*, Usborne

CULTURAL

A Multicultural Guide to Children's Books 0–16+ edited by Rosemary Stones, co-published by BfK and the Reading and Language Centre, Reading
Aesop's Fables 9+, J. Morley, MacDonald
Ancient Egypt Resource Book, J. Mason, Longman
Ancient Greece Resource Book, J. Mason, Longman
An Ocean of Story 8+, MacDonald Young Books
Fairy Tales from India, C. Ness, MacDonald
Celtic Myths 9+, S. McBratney, MacDonald
Creation Stories from Around the World, A. Pilling, Heinemann
Dragons and Monsters 8+, A. Ganeri, MacDonald
Encounters Resource Book (the Aztecs), J. Mason, Longman
Festivals of the World – *Mexico; Germany; India; Israel*, Heinemann Festivals Through the Year 6+, Heinemann
Greek Heroes and Monsters, J. Mason, Longman
Greek Legends 10+, P. Connolly, MacDonald
Greek Myths 9+, J. Morley, MacDonald
Greek Myths and Legends 8+, A. Masters, MacDonald
Living in History Pack, Heinemann
Norse Myths 8+, K. Crossley-Holland, MacDonald
Myths and Legends 8+, Belitha Press
Peoples and Customs of the World 8+, J. Dineen/R. Ingpen, Belitha Press
Native American Tales, Saviour Pirotta, Wayland

POEMS

Poems for a wide variety of cultures and traditions include:
Oxford Book of Animal Poems, Let's Celebrate, Oxford University Press
Rainbow Bird, J. Souhami, Frances Lincoln
Rama and the Demon King, J. Souhami, Frances Lincoln
Roman Myths and Legends 8+, A. Masters, MacDonald
Snapping Turtle Guide to Early Civilisations, Ticktock Publishing Ltd
The Leopard's Drum, J. Souhami, Frances Lincoln

The Tomb of Tutankhaman, J. Mason, Longman
The Willow Pattern Story, A. Drummond, North-South Books
Walker Myths and Legends Packs 7+, Heinemann
Where the Wild Things Are, M. Sendak, Picture Lions

BIG BOOKS

A Collection of Classic Poems 8–9, various authors, Pelican
Ancient Egypt 8–9, James Mason, Pelican
An Introduction to A Midsummer Night's Dream 10–11, L. Marsh, Pelican
An Encyclopaedia of Greek and Roman Gods and Heroes 9–10, Brian Moses, Chiver Press
   Ltd
Entertainers 4–11, Heinemann
Festivals 8–9, J. Ely, Pelican
Musical Instruments of the World 5+ *Flutes; Percussion; Strings; Woodwind and Brass*,
   B. Carson Turner/J. See, Belitha Press
Perseus 10+, Heinemann
Planet of the Robots 8–9, D. Orme, Pelican
Story Poems, various authors, Pelican
Theseus and the Minotaur, H. Eyles, Pelican

USEFUL ADDRESSES

CARN (Classroom Action Research Network) http://www.uea.ac.uk/care/carn/
The Bookcase, 27 Main Street, Lowdham, Nottingham NG14 7AB

INTERNET SITES

The following collection of Internet sites will provide starting points. Links within these sites will enable teachers and children to collate pieces of music for singing and listening as well as many other practical classroom ideas. The list of books will also assist with building repertoire and music-making ideas for the classroom. This list is published on the Internet from John Childs' website: www.john.childs.btinternet.co.uk with the facility to click on links to all the listed sites. All sites contain free information and most have pictures, sound and midi files and demo programs, which are also free.

Bayside Net Midi Collection   http://www.bayside.net/webdev/mindex.htm

Homework Elephant   http://www.homeworkelephant.free-online.co.uk/music.html

Indian Classical Music   http://www.aoe.vt.edu/~boppe/MUSIC/music.html

Instrument Index   http://www.mediaport.net/Music/Instruments/index.en.html

Japanese Musical Instruments   http://www.mhs.mendocino.k12.ca.us/MenComNet/
   Business/Retail/Larknet/Japan

John Childs   http://www.john.childs.btinternet.co.uk/publish/index.html

The Learning Circle   http://www.qca.org.uk/menu.htm

Midi Karaoki files   http://mp3.about.com/cntcrtainmcnt/mp3/gi/dynamic/offsitc.htm?
site=http://www.midikaraoke.com/home/

MP3-Midi Music   http://mp3.about.com/entertainment/mp3/mbody.htm

Music Education for Young Children   http://www.2-life.com/meyc/

National Grid for Learning   http://www.official-documents.co.uk/document/ofsted/
ped/ped.htm

The Orff Society [UK]   http://www.catan.demon.co.uk/orff/

A Review of Primary Education   http://www.official-documents.co.uk/document/ofsted/
ped/ped.htm

School Zone   http://www.schoolzone.co.uk/

Sonic Arts Network   http://www.sonicartsnetwork.org/main_index.html

Study Web – Music   http://www.studyweb.com/

World Music Midi Files   http://www.mediaport.net/Music/Midi/index.fr.html

APPLICATIONS

Cakewalk (Free demo sequencer and notational packages that will allow you to play midi
files and see the notation on screen.)   http://www.cakewalk.com/

Real Player (Free program which will play audio and video clips.)   http://www.real.com/

CD-ROM

Encarta CD-ROM
Hutchinson Encyclopedia of Music CD-ROM
CD-pluscore Schott Music

Further Reading

Allen, A. and Coley, J. (1995) *Dance for All*, 3 vols. London: David Fulton Publishers.

Binns, T. (1994) *Children Making Music*. Hemel Hempstead: Simon and Schuster.

Bloomfield, A. (ed.) (1998) *The Artistic Experience*. Aspects of Education No. 55, University of Hull.

Callaway, G. and Kear, M. (1999) *Teaching Art and Design in the Primary School*. London: David Fulton Publishers.

Childs, J. (1996) *Making Music Special*. London: David Fulton Publishers.

Clark, V. (1990) *Music Through Topics*. Cambridge: Cambridge University Press.

DfEE & QCA (1999) *The National Curriculum Handbook for Primary Teachers in England. Key Stages 1 and 2*. London: DfEE & QCA.

Froebel, F. (1909) *Pedagogics of the Kindergarten*. New York: Appleton.

Gardiner, H. (1989) *Frames of Mind: The Theory of Multiple Intelligences*. New York: Basic Books.

Gilbert, J. (1981) *Musical Starting Points*. London: Ward Lock Educational.

Laban, R. (1948) *Modern Educational Dance*. London: Macdonald and Evans.

National Advisory Committee on Creative and Cultural Education (1999) *All Our Futures – Creativity, Culture and Education*. London: Department for Education and Employment.

National Curriculum Music Working Group (1995) *Teaching Music in the National Curriculum*. Oxford: Heinemann.

Ridgley, S. and Mole, G. (1997) *Sing It and Say It 7*. Woodford Green: International Music Publications Ltd.

Rolfe, L. and Harlow, M. (1997) *Let's Look at Dance*. London: David Fulton Publishers.

Sedgwick, F. (1993) *The Expressive Arts*. London: David Fulton Publishers.

Smith-Autard, J. (1994) *The Art of Dance in Education*. London: A & C Black.

The National Curriculum Handbook for Primary Teachers in England (2000) www.nc.uk.net

Winston, J. (2000) *Drama, Literacy and Moral Education 5–11*. London: David Fulton Publishers.

Index